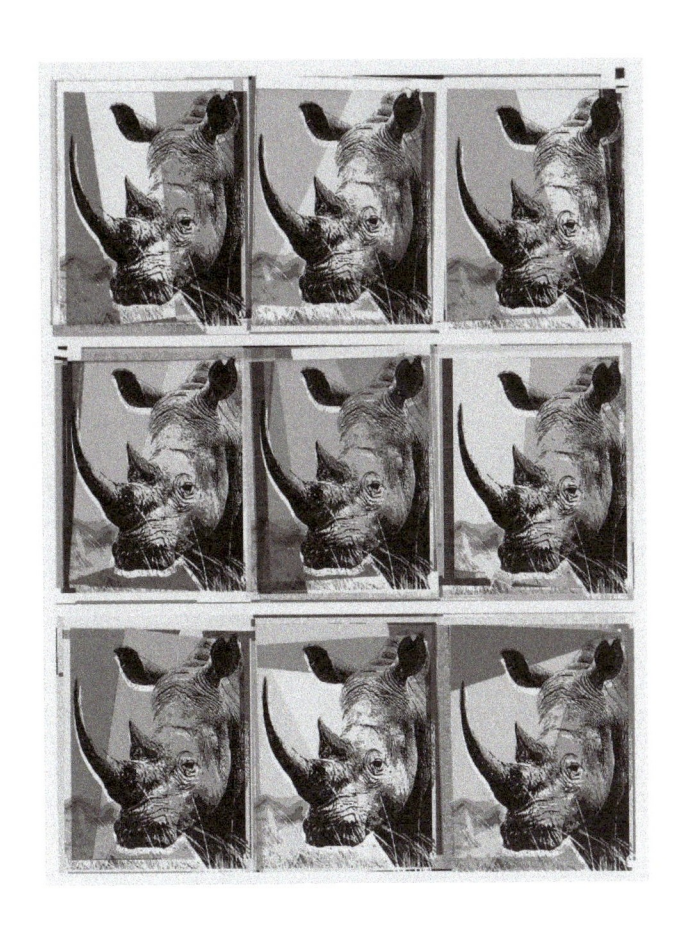

RHINO 2021

RHINO: The Poetry Forum, Inc. is
supported in part by grants from the
Illinois Arts Council, a state agency;
Poets & Writers, Inc.; and
The MacArthur Funds for Arts & Culture
at The Richard H. Driehaus Foundation.

MacArthur Foundation   DRIEHAUS FOUNDATION   ILLINOIS ARTS COUNCIL AGENCY

RHINO is published annually and
considers submissions of poetry, flash fiction/
short-shorts, and translations.
Regular reading period: March 1 to June 15,
or until monthly caps are reached.
Founders' Prize reading period: August 1 to September 30,
or until monthly caps are reached.

Address all correspondence to:

RHINO * P.O. Box 591
Evanston, Illinois 60204
Include SASE
or
editors@rhinopoetry.org

RHINO strongly encourages electronic
submissions. Consult rhinopoetry.org
for details. For those submitting via
the postal service, please include
an SASE for response.

RHINO 2021 is available for $15,
plus postage; back issues are also available.
To order, visit our website,
or send check or money order
to the P.O. address.

Our website features *RHINO Reviews*, as well as
excerpts from past and current issues, events, audio
poems, poet interviews, and prize-winning
poems from our annual Editors' Prizes
and Founders' Prize Contest.
(See inside back cover for details.)
rhinopoetry.org

ISBN: 978-1-945000-04-1
ISSN: 1521-8414

© 2021, *RHINO*: The Poetry Forum, Inc.

All rights to material in this journal revert to
individual authors after *RHINO* publication.

EDITORS
Virginia Bell
Jan Bottiglieri
Jacob Saenz

SENIOR EDITORS
Darren Angle
Ann Hudson
Angela Narciso Torres
Nick Tryling

MANAGING EDITOR
Jan Bottiglieri

ASSOCIATE EDITORS
Carol H. Eding
Naoko Fujimoto
Michael Garza
Gail Goepfert
Kimberly Dixon-Mays
John McCarthy
Beth McDermott
Elizabeth O'Connell-Thompson
Daniel Suárez
Donna Vorreyer

RHINO REVIEWS EDITOR
Angela Narciso Torres

TRANSLATION INITIATIVE EDITOR
Naoko Fujimoto

OUTREACH EDITOR
Kenyatta Rogers

EDITORIAL ASSISTANT READER
Kathryn Bick

SUMMER READING FELLOWS
Noh Anothai
Nestor Gomez

INTERNS
Laura Evers
Michael O'Rear
Dove Rebmann
Erin Sutherlin
Khyla Wallace

BOARD
Ralph Hamilton (Chair)
Laura Cohen
Albert DeGenova
Joanne Diaz
Adam Green
Valerie Wallace

CREDITS
Design by David Syrek; cover design by Darren Angle
Illustration by Sarah Kaiser-Amaral
Page number ornament by David Lee Csicsko
Production by Godfrey Carmona

CONTENTS

Editors' Note	x	
Editors' Prizes	xii	
Founders' Prizes	xiv	
Endre Ady	*On New Waters I Sail* Translated from the Hungarian by Paul Sohar	1
Kelli Russell Agodon	*The world is full of lists of animals that keep disappearing*	2
Anthony Aguero	*Everyone Wants to Tell Me How to Be Alone*	3
Rennie Ament	*Tough*	4
Yvonne Amey	*Two Baby Armadillos*	5
Beck Anson	*Balancing Act*	6
Rose Auslander	*Sun pale as the moon*	7
Wale Ayinla	*The Ending of Things*	8
Jamaica Baldwin	*Father Weaver*	9
Jamaica Baldwin	*Breast/Less*	10
Abbigail Baldys	*Channel Study: A Critical Discourse on the Law of Connection — Abstract*	13
Marie-Claire Bancquart	*Of Man* Translated from the French by Claire Eder and Marie Moulin-Salles	14
Marie-Claire Bancquart	*Outside of* Translated from the French by Claire Eder and Marie Moulin-Salles	16
Caroline Barnes	*To My Sister's Wheelchair*	17
Francesca Bell	*Truth Is*	19
Monica Berlin	*Quarantime, Day 164*	20
Monica Berlin	*Quarantime, Day 38*	22
Sheila Black	*The Piling Up of Strange Days*	23
Adrian Blevins	*Get, Little Poem, Little Shoelace Between Death & Me,*	25
Sarah Browning	*Monday Morning*	26
Chris Campanioni	*kaze no denwa*	27
Sarah Carson	*No One in This Dumb Bar Will Acknowledge How Famous We Are*	30
Anne Champion	*Match Girl*	31
Anne Champion	*Why Didn't You Tell Anyone?*	32
Sean Cho A.	*Waiting on the Next End*	35
Lisa Compo	*A Conjuration for My Daily 4pm Creature*	36
Britny Cordera	*Herbarium*	38
Phillip J. Cozzi	*The Fabric Anthology of Green*	40

Curtis L. Crisler	Fifty Something Years of ~~Letters~~ Laters	41
Jessica Cuello	The Sitters	45
Leia Darwish	Notes (In Retrograde)	46
Elisabeth Reidy Denison	The Student Considers the Hyacinth Girl	47
Brandon Thomas DiSabatino	"open all night."	48
Aline Dolinh	Still Life with Beheaded Chicken	49
Lara Egger	How to Operate Under Normal Conditions	50
Michael Frazier	The Japanese Characters for Kindness are 親切 Meaning Parent and Cut	51
Michael Frazier	Irrational Fear of Home	52
Elizabeth Galoozis	Black and White	55
Adam Gianforcaro	Fever Dream as Cardio	56
Jessica Goodfellow	Lumen	57
Hayley Graffunder	Doomsday Baby & I	59
Hayley Graffunder	Doom & the Elephant in the Room	61
Benjamin S. Grossberg	Imaginary Litter Boxes with Real Cats in Them	62
Kathleen Hellen	On white appearance of a wall	64
Ambalila Hemsell	Fire Season	65
Maura High	Still Life	66
Excell N. Hunter	Sobbing Sky I See You	67
Korey Hurni	On the Pacific Coast Highway	69
Adeeko Ibukun	Night Cabaret	70
Rebecca Irene	Insufficient	71
Nazifa Islam	Fortunes	72
Kenneth Jakubas	Letter Constructing a Face	73
Susan Johnson	And I Ask You America	74
Michal "MJ" Jones	"I Always Wanted to Bang A Black Boi"	74
Aseem Kaul	Clearing the air	74
Rogan Kelly	Your Jazz Mouth All Over Monday Morning	77
David Keplinger	Birthday	78
Chris Ketchum	Powerline	79
Ashley Sojin Kim	Last Frost	81
Kathleen Kirk	Death of a Sasquatch	82
emilie kneifel	Dreaming	83
Susanna Lang	Poste Restante	84
Scot Langland	Triolet Grief	87
Mariana Lin	One Night in Melchior Islands	91

CONTENTS

Christopher Locke	*Counting*	92
Anthony Thomas Lombardi	*upon hearing Prince sing "Purple Rain" at First Avenue in Minneapolis in 1983, I begin to understand my mother's love life*	93
Tara Mesalik MacMahon	*Did You Know Paradise Means*	95
Angie Macri	*Elegy*	96
Elizabeth Majerus	*If You Are a White Person*	97
Robert McDonald	*Irruption*	99
Steve McDonald	*Lesson*	102
T.J. McLemore	*Anthroposcenes*	103
Claire McQuerry	*Transaction*	104
David Melville	*Tohubohu*	107
Henri Meschonnic	*[all of life]* Translated from the French by Don Boes and Gabriella Bedetti	109
Robin Messing	*Song of My Exile*	110
Aksinia Mihaylova	*The Word* Translated from the French by Marissa Davis	111
Amy Miller	*Camera*	112
Rebecca Morton	*Everything I'd Ever Seen*	113
Simone Muench & Jackie K. White	*Self-Portrait Lined by Anna Akhmatova*	115
Jason Myers	*On Learning Langston Hughes Wanted His Funeral to End with "Do Nothin' Til You Hear From Me"*	116
Kell Nelson	*For the Union Dead*	118
Sarah Nichols	*A*PTSD (Android Post Traumatic Stress Disorder): Bernard*	119
Brianna Noll	*How Far Can a Memory Be Trusted?*	121
Colleen O'Brien	*Moving*	122
Cindy Juyoung Ok	*Curtain*	124
Sara Lupita Olivares	*Interruptions*	125
Christina Olson	*Reptile House*	126
Pablo Otavalo	*Vigil*	128
Rachelle Parker	*Echoes of Coarse Fabric*	130
Genevieve Payne	*At Georgia's House Party*	131
Cecilia Pinto	*[Joyous]*	132
Cecilia Pinto	*Nurse*	134
Megan Pinto	*Seascape with Father*	135
Susan Azar Porterfield	*J.M.W. Turner, Slavers Throwing overboard the Dead and Dying—Typhoon coming on*	136

Meg Reynolds	*We Are Happy*	137
Rainer Maria Rilke	*Buddha* Translated from the German by Donald Mace Williams	138
Liana Sakelliou	*The Italian Circus on the Moraitiki Shore* Translated from the Greek by Don Schofield	139
Liana Sakelliou	*Marine Education at the Beginning of the Twentieth Century* Translated from the Greek by Don Schofield	140
Stewart Shaw	*Plants and Trees*	141
Carrie Shipers	*Performance Review: "You seem to really struggle with the culture here"*	142
Sarah Dickenson Snyder	*Entering The Odyssey*	144
Jennifer Sperry Steinorth	*Her Read*	145
Noah Stetzer	*A Two-Body Problem*	155
Keli Stewart	*How to Read Tea Leaves*	157
Keli Stewart	*on turning 30*	158
Stephanie Lane Sutton	*Palindromes*	159
Jason Tandon	*Writing*	160
Maya Tevet Dayan	*Cotton* Translated from the Hebrew by Jane Medved	161
Lee Colin Thomas	*Stride*	163
Cedric Tillman	*Feed My People (The Toxicology Prayer)*	165
Rodrigo Toscano	*The Revolution*	166
Jess Turner	*In The Acred Woods*	168
Stephen Tuttle	*Elijah Fed by Ravens*	170
Enrique S. Villasis	*Muro Ami* Translated from Filipino by Bernard Capinpin	171
Sara Moore Wagner	*How to Survive It*	172
John Sibley Williams	*Self-Portrait as Lacuna*	173
Daniel Woody	*euphemisms*	175
William Winfield Wright	*Evaporation*	176
Brandon Young	*Held Me Green and Dying*	178
Emily Zogbi	*I Help Lara Croft With Her First Kill*	180

Contributors' Notes	183
Donors	198
Founders' Prize Information	inside back cover

EDITORS' NOTE

Welcome to RHINO Poetry's 45th print issue, coming on the heels of an historic year. Indeed, when the speaker in Claudia Rankine's *Don't Let Me Be Lonely* (2004) claims that "what alerts, alters," we want to believe it. More than ever in 2021, we want to believe human consciousness is capable of beauty and justice. We even believe that an anagram—"alerts" into "alters"—is a spark of possibility and potentiality. Wordplay, a cornerstone of poetry, is potent and necessary work.

RHINO Poetry felt the intensity of the past year and responded. We began by celebrating Ralph Hamilton's 12-year tenure as Editor-in-Chief and his new position as Chairperson of the Board, and we transitioned to a new editorial masthead. Our free Poetry Forum workshops and RHINO Reads! series moved online, becoming accessible to audiences both local and remote. To support the work of BIPOC-identified poets, we curated the online project #RHINOPoetryforBlackLives and launched the RHINO archive project, #RHINOart2art. We continue to publish the acclaimed online series RHINO Reviews, curated by Angela Narciso Torres, and featuring micro-reviews of poetry, prose, and translation, with graphic and video iterations.

For this year's Founders' Contest, we recruited nationally esteemed, award-winning poet Ed Roberson as guest judge. And we gathered poems for this issue that range in content and style, but always seize our attention with their potent, necessary, and often timely work. Here is a sample of what you will find in these pages:

I wake knowing I've been stumbling past my death-place
for years   I wish my father was here
We could dive into the part of the ocean where it's always dark
he'd point out the light hanging above an angler fish's mouth

~ Sean Cho A.

If he wasn't janitor he'd be gravel artist, he'd be glitter farmer, he'd groove skate
down beach hill to Isley Brothers. If he wasn't janitor he'd be tennis racketeer,
ocean tamer, cicada sequencer, he'd turn his knit cap upside down to catch fire

~ Jamaica Baldwin

like the Jamaican caper overgrown
on the side of a narrow tropical road,
its fragile male and female parts sprawling
forth from a metal barricade

~ Britny Cordera

The point was never the transmission of meaning. The point is only ever to get it down. Or: to let it rise up.

~ Chris Campanioni

A NOTE ON THE COVER ART & DESIGN:

For this year's new cover, designed by Darren Angle, we are thankful for the reproduction of "Permeable Boundaries" by acclaimed visual artist Sarah Kaiser-Amaral. This cover represents a move toward a more associative understanding of what "RHINO" stands for: creative work that provokes thought and pushes the boundaries in form and feeling, while connecting with our readers and audience.

We invite you to read Kaiser-Amaral's statement about "Permeable Boundaries" and the connection between visual art and poetry in 2021:

Boundaries can be physical wires or fences that divide property or territory. Some barriers keep us safe inside by keeping intruders out. Some barriers are used to exclude or to cage, to enact violence on others. Boundaries can also be imaginary lines that we have been told not to cross. I was raised in a blended family, in that I was a stepchild, and now live in a blended family, as the stepmother. I have sometimes felt like an outsider in my own home.

On a larger scale, the written and "unwritten" laws of boundaries hurt many families, hurt communities of color and non-conforming genders, hurt all of us, in the end. And in the midst of the pandemic, boundaries are asserted now more than ever. We wear masks to protect ourselves from others, and to protect others from ourselves. We social distance, and coexist within our little bubbles and pods, unless we do not have the privilege of isolation. We greet loved ones through screens. Our nation is polarized — politically divided. Consequently, we often feel quite isolated, and very much alone. Art and poetry are one way to speak to each other, to reach across boundaries, to forge a connection, however fragile, however ephemeral, however we can.

RALPH HAMILTON EDITORS' PRIZES 2021

FIRST PRIZE

Father Weaver
by
Jamaica Baldwin

SECOND PRIZE

Feed My People (The Toxicology Prayer)
by
Cedric Tillman

HONORABLE MENTION

Irrational Fear of Home
by
Michael Frazier

TRANSLATION PRIZE

Cotton
by
Maya Tevet Dayan
Translated from the Hebrew by Jane Medved

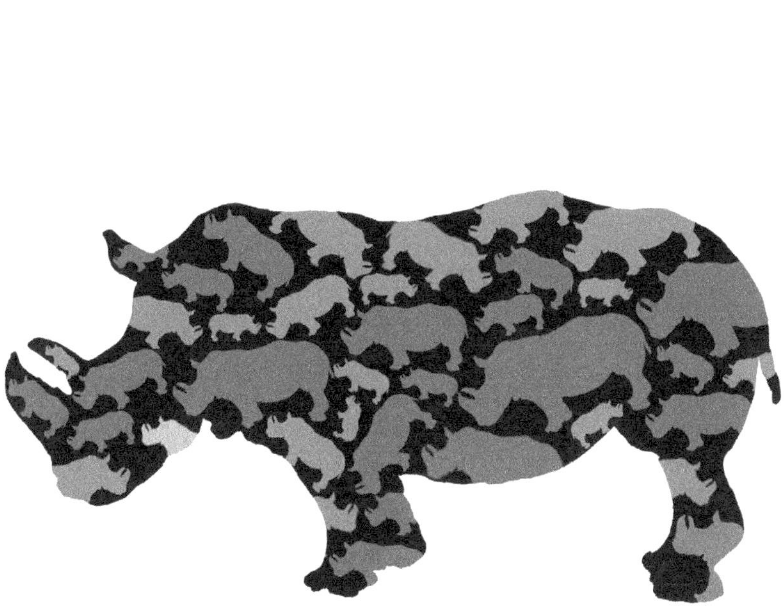

FOUNDERS' PRIZES 2021

FIRST PRIZE

Fifty Something Years of ~~Letters~~ Laters—
my paradoxical absolution of Emmett Till
by
Curtis L. Crisler

RUNNERS-UP

Quarantime, Day 164
by
Monica Berlin

The Sitters
by
Jessica Cuello

In addition, we selected contest poems by the following
poets for publication in this issue of *RHINO*:

Kelli Russell Agodon	TJ McLemore
Beck Anson	Amy Miller
Caroline Barnes	Simone Muench
Monica Berlin	Cindy Joyoung Ok
Anne Champion	Christina Olson
Lisa Compo	Pablo Otavalo
Phillip Cozzi	Rachelle Parker
Elisabeth Reidy Denison	Megan Pinto
Lara Egger	Susan Azar Porterfield
Michael Frazier	Stewart Shaw
Elizabeth Galoozis	Noah Stetzer
Aseem Kaul	Keli Stewart
Chris Ketchum	Frederick Tillman
Kathleen Kirk	Rodrigo Toscano
Yuxi Lin	Jackie K. White
Elizabeth Majurus	John Sibley Williams
Robert McDonald	William Wright

Information on next year's contest can be found
on the inside back cover and at rhinopoetry.org.

Endre Ady
Translated from the Hungarian by Paul Sohar

On New Waters I Sail
(*Új vizeken járok*)

Have no fear, my ship, tomorrow is on board,
The jeering mob can't keep this drunken oarsman moored.
Ride the waves, my ship,
Have no fear, my ship: tomorrow is on board.

To go on flying, flying on and on and on
To great new Waters, virgin Waters, like a swan,
Ride the waves, my ship,
To go on flying, flying on and on and on.

New horizons are arising to caress your eyes,
Every minute mounts a whole new Paradise,
Ride the waves, my ship,
New horizons are arising to caress your eyes.

To hell with all old rancid dreams already dreamt,
On waves of new pains, secrets, and thirsts I'm sent,
Ride the waves, my ship,
To hell with all old rancid dreams already dreamt.

I'll never be a fiddler of the market place,
Whether driven by wine or a holy face:
Ride the waves, my ship,
I'll never be a fiddler of the market place.

Kelli Russell Agodon

The world is full of lists of animals that keep disappearing

and I find myself at a sanctuary
with a baby giraffe who was rejected
by his mother and displaced
by a hurricane in Texas. I have never
been so close to something so wild.
As I pet its neck, the giraffe chirps
like a small bird waiting in its nest
for its mother to return, mother
earth, mother ship, motherboard,
mother bored with her son next to me
who keeps trying to find the perfect
round stone on the ground
of the sanctuary and I almost laugh
at that term, *sanctuary*: what we call
places we created to save what we have
injured—*refuge, shelter, safehaven*,
and I look around and see nothing is
safe here, like how everything is
beautiful until you see the scuffs
on the walls, the story of something
so wild not wanting to be held in.

Anthony Aguero

Everyone Wants to Tell Me How to Be Alone

Wrong place. Wrong time. How to settle
for the wrong dream. Wrong wrist.
Wrong preference. Wrong skin.
Diving into the seawater that is really
a river. Wrong space. Wrong degree.
Wrong way of rolling r's. Wrong size.
Something created to read from right
to left. Wrong way to love. Wrong,
wrong disease. Wrong drugs. Wrong
choice of words. The way he was
gentle with me is what you need to do.
Try again. Wrong breath.
Wrong embrace. Wrong smell. Wrong
choices. How to wake up correctly.
How to cough up river water onto the
Wrong place.

Rennie Ament

Tough

I had just come through the door. I had come from a spa weekend. I had just come from the doctor who had told me I had eggs. I had just received the news I would die of amateur knitting. I had climbed in through the window. I was waiting for myself to get back from drifting like pollen on the wind. Which is a weather thing. A thing is not alive, I think. This could be very wrong. I had just come from the cellar. There were many ghosts downstairs. But I had wanted a potato. A tiny automata. I had wanted to have children. But the world was not waiting for more people. People are doomed to sit and think. So whom do I sit and think to. The world. A thing. Which has the task of spinning in ether. I had come home from the cold night air. My body felt like a megaton crystal. How I wished to be a crystal. How I wanted a potato.

Yvonne Amey

Two Baby Armadillos

a mirror looks like you don't want to look like you
never look into mirrors you don't want to see you
then how do you love yourself or even change you
there are mirrors in your mansion that dither you
in the dining room living room four large ones you
have a few antique hand-helds in the bathroom you
have met ones in cars into the forest-front-yard you
with your Nikon watch two baby armadillos you
witness them root through loose rot one looks at you
are afraid you continue spying at asymmetrical you
nod to the brown bark on trunks of trees you
allow weeds to shoot between your two shoes you
inside this tree-evening you
brown-edge of weed this thicket is within you

Beck Anson

Balancing Act

There wasn't a warning label
for the confused looks, or the stares,
or the whispers from the other side
of the bathroom stall. Just —
wash hands with soap and water
before and after injection.

It's a balancing act, really.
Each milligram absorbed
moves the slider across the beam
tipping the scale ever so slightly
in the direction of other.
The funny part is
I didn't set the calibration.
So I do the arithmetic, adding and subtracting —

+ 1	chin stubble	
- 1	soft jawline	
+ 1	thigh hair	
- 1	wide hips	
+ 1	happy trail	
- 1	menstrual blood	
+ 1	heightened desire	(to fuck)
- 1	tears	

  0   me, imperfectly balanced,
            imperfectly whole.

Rose Auslander

Sun pale as the moon

here on Sea Street, car heater
blasting, windows shut, virus masks in our laps,
dying to throw off our clothes and swim—
him eating a burger, me licking a cone
wishing it had sprinkles, snow
starting to stick on the beach,
the wind chasing reeds
by the rusting lifeguard chair,
bending them in waves, gray gold
catching weak bits of light & oh
here it is, the grease from his fries
& the melting ice cream tastes like July.
                     & those nights when he coughs
& I can't sleep, why is it this
I long for, not summer, floating together
buoyant in dark water, feet snagging
long strands of seaweed & almost not caring,
but these semi-frozen waves, someone's dog
slipping on the ice, the clouds looking for stars
under sand & crusty snow, the half-empty cup
wedged in the rocks, the two gulls cawing
on a mattress in the dumpster.

Wale Ayinla

The Ending of Things

to tell a story about gratitude, to tell it as your chest erupts
into a lamplight. with chrysanthemum in the chest. to engage
the departure of the body's habitant. and also, you are an ascent
of wrinkles. paper-like turbulence. the cloud over your head
sets itself on fire. its ash is boxed on your tongue. you unfather
the evening from your skin; your body is now an unsteady deluge
unbuckling its menace. delirium, possible gifting.
you have the knowledge of shimmering waters made into crows.
of people, mostly. petrichor of names returning as hunger.
the mouth is having more than enough to chew into tenderness.
being a custodian of losses, a headstone bearing the names of strangers.
a monument carved like the eyes of a bird. facing every direction
with a capitalized transcription of grief. the letterings are pledging
allegiance. still, here is the gravel tossed inside a conglomeration
of tongues rendered to silence. a castaway.
—to a house outweighed by silent prayers.
—to a song slapping the face of the river for harmony.
—to a tree lifting God's face on its shoulders.
—to the birds whose wings are clipped by loss.
—to the road made grey into a rock.
—to the soul tired of traveling back to its shredding space.
—to the naked wind of repetition spread as a mother's embrace.
—to the lament in every weary footstep. the sand smothering.
—to the heart still unmarked by inkblots of miracles.
—to the prison in the smile, the abundance of light on the lintel of the mouth.
—to the happiness pitched in the history of sadness, the dream of moths.
—to the ruins, and the body polished with desolation.

Jamaica Baldwin

Father Weaver

If he wasn't janitor he'd be gravel artist, he'd be glitter farmer, he'd groove skate
down beach hill to Isley Brothers. If he wasn't janitor he'd be tennis racketeer,
ocean tamer, cicada sequencer, he'd turn his knit cap upside down to catch fire

flies, load them into pitching machine, point upwards and shoot stars into sky.
If he hadn't been liquor undertaker, booze regulator, drunk-gambling-wish denier
he might have been daughter wrangler, fear whisperer, sweet lullaby impersonator.

His under-water voice might have sung me to float and swell. If he hadn't been vodka
foreman he might have used strands of daughter hair to draw maps of blackness
on his body. I might have watched them stretch and curve and maze him into father

quest into secret daughter mission. I'd pack a flashlight and three meals per day.
I'd stretch and nimble get. I'd compass take, whistle and song and song. I'd path
follow and lost get and around turn, around turn till I center reach and undead him.

Jamaica Baldwin

Breast/Less

The nestle of fingers
        entwined with
                                other fingers
    milk thistle   capsules breaking
                        open blood

        coagulating   pages of a book
                        unturned pigment-

   stained finger nails
            bones losing
 density
     a remembered song
                                 unsung
                           stuck
 on a word   a thought
      things that have nothing

                        in common

but the sound
       they don't make
           loving a word

     for itself   not

for its meaning:
                 crest-fallen
                 philistine
                 ingratiate

       loving the meaning

                                                                               but not the word:

pulchritude
bucolic
intercourse
                sex

                even that
                                  nipples offering

                themselves up
                                              to tongue   to lips
                                                      to fingers

            nipples that will never
            offer
                            themselves up again—

                like mine
                words

                            whose sound and meaning
                            I love

                            and hate:

                                                mamilla
                                                teat
                                                udder
                                                licentious

the absurdity of everything
                                          that doesn't make me

Jamaica Baldwin

    salivate
    cum
    cackle
    moan

                            a paper towel soaked in turpentine
                            resting on the edge of a waste basket

          airing itself
            not combusting into flame not burning this place to the ground not this
hot flash not from sex or that novel about bondage everyone's read but me pages unturned
inches and inches
untouched   flammable   wickless matchless.

Marie-Claire Bancquart
Translated from the French by Claire Eder and
Marie Moulin-Salles

Of Man

In a storm-distorted sky
the sea walks
with the heavy cliff.

Brief flash
hangs
in a scent of ozone and rain on the waters.

Land without compassion or fault

unbearably serene.

In heart: another cycle of being
our masts our chimneys
advertisement on a building
the arteries in us
all our dated ephemera
that aromatizes blood for the impassive angel of night.

Don't press these fierce fingers
so hastily into the shoulder of the landscape.

It eludes us
thin memory at a gallop
dragging its seaweed
through our bodies, subtly estranged from birds.

Our space
doesn't star the sky.

Abbigail Baldys

Channel Study: A Critical Discourse on the Law of Connection — *Abstract*

Remember the screen   *connection—feeling*   your photograph
held there, surrounded   a forest   holding an overgrown meadow, disassembling, the grass
green tongues   *pull fire through*
the leaves, this forest   *being drawn*
a channel of it, soundless and gentle and falsely nostalgic like saying
'I think I know you.'   'I think I've known you before.'   Remember
the building, two of us inside it, standing in ourselves   *toward one another*   speaking
about the man who was skiing, who crashed into the pines, we were   *being drawn*
speaking about him: *together—*   we had been him, were him in that loss
of control—   the circle our feet draw by the pond   *occurs rhythmically*
remember pebbles, banks,   water refuses to wash, me   *in every day human social experience*
you   *a critical happening*   smoking on the trunk of your car   *machine*   *carries us*
border to border   our separations   *this experience opens us to*   *glances*
I exchange with the screen   *complex interstices*   as if you're there, a weight
my hand fails to measure like inordinate gold;   remember I am surrounded
by you   *in, of, and between consciousnesses*   escape offers no postures   to fold my body through, I
sprawl out among fiery light   *with whom we interact*   and give my form   *this study examines*   to branches
folding down   *connection's potential energies—*   the actual   *mystical, mythical—*   contours your body
pushes against space, against me   climbing the streets   *and investigates*   when the two-ness we claim disappears
like the forest knocked over on the hill,   wounded dirt a deep stain   *their cultivation:*
crashing between us   *ultimately, the bonds we form*   into our sound
that grows nothing like distance   *can be practiced—*   hum of blood,
of nerves,   *can be disciplined to resolve*   blue like a tower
remembers: our channels   *fragmented need*   indefensible sky

Abbigail Baldys

Channel Study: A Critical Discourse on the Law of Connection — *Abstract*

Remember the screen   *connection—feeling*   your photograph
held there, surrounded   *a forest*   holding an overgrown meadow, disassembling, the grass
green tongues   *pull fire through*
the leaves, this forest   *being drawn*
a channel of it, soundless and gentle and falsely nostalgic like saying
'I think I know you.'   'I think I've known you before.'   Remember
the building, two of us inside it, standing in ourselves   *toward one another*   speaking
about the man who was skiing, who crashed into the pines, we were   *being drawn*
speaking about him: *together—*   we had been him, were him in that loss
of control—   the circle our feet draw by the pond   *occurs rhythmically*
remember pebbles, banks,   water refuses to wash, me   *in every day human social experience*
you   *a critical happening*   smoking on the trunk of your car   *machine*   carries us
border to border   *our separations*   *this experience opens us to*   *glances*
I exchange with the screen   *complex interstices*   as if you're there, a weight
my hand fails to measure like inordinate gold;   remember I am surrounded
by you   *in, of, and between consciousnesses*   escape offers no postures   to fold my body through, I
sprawl out among fiery light   *with whom we interact*   and give my form   *this study examines*   to branches
folding down   *connection's potential energies—*   the actual   *mystical, mythical—*   contours your body
pushes against space, against me   climbing the streets   *and investigates*   when the two-ness we claim disappears
like the forest knocked over on the hill,   wounded dirt a deep stain   *their cultivation:*
crashing between us   *ultimately, the bonds we form*   into our sound
that grows nothing like distance   *can be practiced—*   hum of blood,
of nerves,   *can be disciplined to resolve*   blue like a tower
remembers: our channels   *fragmented need*   indefensible sky

Marie-Claire Bancquart
Translated from the French by Claire Eder and
Marie Moulin-Salles

Of Man

In a storm-distorted sky
the sea walks
with the heavy cliff.

Brief flash
hangs
in a scent of ozone and rain on the waters.

Land without compassion or fault

unbearably serene.

In heart: another cycle of being
our masts our chimneys
advertisement on a building
the arteries in us
all our dated ephemera
that aromatizes blood for the impassive angel of night.

Don't press these fierce fingers
so hastily into the shoulder of the landscape.

It eludes us
thin memory at a gallop
dragging its seaweed
through our bodies, subtly estranged from birds.

Our space
doesn't star the sky.

A shadow between womb and memory
serves as a passage for strangers
emerged from waves.

Then a stunning sustenance:
the pleasure of living slaps the outside the inside.

The land passes through our mouths
like a finger through a wedding ring.

Marie-Claire Bancquart
Translated from the French by Claire Eder and
Marie Moulin-Salles

Outside of

Infinitive and soft
tree talk
harvest of sap in the earth.

Between resin and blood
the sun sweetened by leaves
filters a long dream over the verbs
whispered
without past or future
a faultless gesture:
to drink
to live
to fuse your body with pine needles.

Lying halfway outside of yourself
you're the echo of a tree's contentment.

Caroline Barnes

To My Sister's Wheelchair

We bonded over her, worked as a team
those last few weeks. You, a nursing home
workhorse, standard issue, nothing fancy.
Thin vinyl sling seat, no padding, solid

carbon-steel frame. Swing-away footrests,
yes, but no calf supports. Me, a basic sister,
the kind who calls on Sundays but yawns
at mundane chitchat and always has to run.

Decades of this until the falling started,
until she reported fingers too weak to press
the nozzle on her perfume bottle, until
her doctor said this isn't good when pushing

against her forehead to test neck strength.
But we made her happy, didn't we, you and I.
How about the day we found an empty corridor
and raced down it so she could feel a breeze

on her face again? No chance of tipping with
your perfect distribution, your wide tires
so sure of themselves on the polished floor.
Remember how we waited outside the PT room

where they tried to get her on her feet again?
I almost felt you praying too. Your discretion
on the patio when I lit her forbidden cigarette,
and again, the night her wife slipped in unseen

with a bottle of Jack Daniels, how you watched
over them, faithful sentinel, as in the dark their

Caroline Barnes

bodies found the familiar curves of 20 years.
I envy you the way you carry weight, not grief.

When all is done, how a spray and wipe can make
you gleam again. Parked back at Intake, unaware of
those walking out, heads down, carrying their grief
like an armful of clothing no one wants to wear.

Francesca Bell

Truth Is

this body is a body of evidence,
a crime scene never secured.

It is tracked, scuffed.
Dust it, and you'll see all the prints.

This body is losing its grip.

It is no longer anyone's
convenience, no more a sleek
purse stuffed with youth's currency.

More a satchel of regrets,
an old sack steadily unseaming.

When I had the colonoscopy,
they found tiny ulcers blooming
like anemones.

All those bad years, it seems,
I was eating myself
from the inside.
Turns out,

the body cannot lie.

It mangles us in metaphor.
Turns us, weeping, over similes' knees.

No matter how hard
I pretend to be okay,
this body is prostrate,

teaching me to beg.

Monica Berlin

Quarantime, Day 164

Before broken, built. & that's true of
our whole lives & every single part—
of us, what's in us, & what we make, &
what the world makes for us. Before
a tree is taken down by wind shear, by
gale force, by chainsaw, by fire, first
it grew. Before someone on the street
brandishes a long gun, he had to learn
to hold something small in his hand, to
pick up an object, to train his muscles
to recognize weight & size & shape. &
on the street, in his arms, in some other
time, he might've chosen a paintbrush,
trumpet, book, or to reach out empty
handed to a stranger, to sky. & before
hatred, before fear, sensory or sense
maybe. Before language, our bodies
—how we move through a day or don't
move at all. Before words, pulse & breath
& hunger &—. & after, what we return to
before departing, reduced to our elements,
bone & muscle & skin & cell. Sometimes
a storm can take everything down & fast,
without warning or judgment. Sometimes
that undoing slow & unnoticed, one small
fissure after another until topple, until
gives way. Sometimes we can come back
from disaster, repair or rebuild, an after.
Sometimes what's knocked down stays
down. I mean someone built every last

thing & some of it remarkable, & all of it
somehow ours, our responsibility & debt
& burden & sometimes our home &
sometimes what we flee. & after, when
what's built is broken, no matter how or
at what cost or how loved, there is rubble,
a mess, ruin or ruins, something worth some
-thing—to coax back to health, to mend or
patch, to waterproof, to tend, to bury, to
memorialize, to forget, to forgive, to raze
what remains, to repurpose.

Monica Berlin

Quarantime, Day 38

Or call this variation on a theme—that minor chord
elegiac, melancholy, or how shadow casts over
landscape, blues everything. Or note measurement
of time, which is also how we measured before
& will again if there's something that resembles
luck enough. Or skim any record left behind of
our being here, these lines their own return, to find
proof. We've never not been afraid, never not thought
there is nothing to say, never don't remember how
slight any chance. Always brought to our knees, which
is sometimes reaction to sorrow & sometimes to beauty,
to silence or what we'd call holy, which is grief & joy,
which is most of this life—though not its boredom,
tedium, one room to another & back again, not treading
water or treading the same ground, looping our own little
postage stamp, block after block, day after day. Tonight
in the news I don't read, a headline makes clear that we
will forget this time in time, which seems as impossible
as knowing how any of this will end. Which seems
impossible. I mean we don't & aren't likely to, though
the edges will soften, shade. I mean every new day
a day we've not lived before. I mean grief is its own
public square & private corner, memorial to. & time,
time keeps its own archives, catalogue. I mean we will
say we weren't there or we were here or it was like
nothing else or it was somehow familiar. I mean I will
repeat what I always have: that I wasn't there but never
don't wake remembering that others were. I mean tonight
in news I do read I find a series starting to take shape,
nearly the same sentence again & again, different sources,
something about the no-longer-viable if, the flaw of if &
the urgency of when, the certainty of when.

Sheila Black

The Piling Up
of Strange Days

You begin to think about silence
differently.

Perhaps it has dimension, as when you stop
talking to your husband

for a day—it is as if you are giving yourself
permission to visit

another country, or when you move
the computer from desk

to table—one window view to another,
as if you are learning to make

kingdoms of small spaces the way you did
as a child, removing the couch

cushions to make a fort under
the dining room table. Now when you go out

you feel turtle-like—shell-less, soft-bellied,
blinking yet also dazzled.

Why did you never notice how many birds
depend on your fig tree or how

different the red of the common finch
from the red of the common cardinal,

Sheila Black

and what a miracle hummingbirds are
the way they hover and suspend themselves

to drink from the tiny mouths of purple
candle flowers,

the dead monarch trapped in the high grass,
and the plants growing a little more profuse

each and every day. You are forgetting
things—like what day of the week it is or

why you got here; at first you cooked
elaborate meals three times a day. Now you eat

standing up, a raw tomato sliced in half
reamed with sea salt.

Adrian Blevins

Get, Little Poem, Little Shoelace Between Death & Me,

the fuck out of bed & tell the people
how dumb marriage is. How dull & jackass.

How un-rife, but non-stop. Tell them
for love you need no kids for starters

& monstrous swaths like meadows of things
like horizons & moonscapes & skylines to want

& glass buildings & rope ladders
& a faraway beach covered in hummocks of snow

& fields of breeze-rain in the hair & on the roof
& a drawing pad like a humongous white canvas of yes

like flecks of lemon on the lips & not—
just not—the mouth like a hinge of spit

mouthing the end—holy writ, but counterfeit—of it.

Sarah Browning

Monday Morning

It's been two years, my son says
in the car beside me, two blocks
from school. *I'm over it.*

I'm glad, is all I say, though how it is
my sadness and his dad's sadness
don't swamp him I do not know.

You didn't have to do it, he says,
one block from school. *I did*, I say,
I did have to do it. As the light

turns green. But the sun is
in my eyes and he has to tell
me to go. *But still I'm sad*, I say,

as we arrive and as he climbs
his big frame out of the car and
shuts the door and walks toward what is next.

Chris Campanioni

kaze no denwa

I write because I cannot draw the eyelash above your lip, the eyelash floating toward your feet, our feet, as we stand and wait for it, as if we wanted to wait for it to fall, as if we wanted to wait for it to stop falling.

•

(The rain continued all day.)

•

How to tell time from the body. I mean the difference between time and the body, the body and time.

•

I write because I cannot make music. The fingers are right here, in front of the eyes, to gaze at and to touch and be touched. Right in front of the eyes. Whereas the throat is a mystery.

•

(It demands imagination.)

•

A singer, for instance, has an unprotected relationship to their audience. No barrier between their voice entering my body.

•

Chris Campanioni

What I wouldn't do for that kind of immediacy. What I wouldn't do for that kind of involuntary trespass.

•

How to explain diminuendo in a text. The exertion of getting softer. Peristaltic pre-dawn and my face pressed into the carpet. My face pressed into the wooden beams below. The exertion of getting softer. The book as a flight from public.

•

How else how else would I disappear.

•

I am sitting here, like you, sweating. Silent. Like you. To stretch back as far as one can go. And to go farther. Farther or further. An indistinguishable point in the distance. I like places I've never been in person. I like persons I've never been. They say this exercise opens the heart.

•

Like you, I am still waiting for the mouth to drop. Back to something like an original place. As if all things didn't come from all other things; as if everything isn't already elsewhere.

•

On the crowded F train leaning toward home I find your voice beside me: I enjoy reading you in migration, dimming between dark and day, rising above ground and down. I mean south. It is always something I am thinking that puts an end to something I am feeling. But sometimes it also happens the other way.

•

Spaces invent practices. Lest we forget, practices can also invent spaces. I am talking to myself again, but on the train, at least, during the commute, in the middle of day or somewhere in the middle … so many possibilities for reaching out, or for being touched, or for nothing else but listening.

●

There are things not meant to be seen, not meant to be sorted or sorted out.

●

I wanted to write about a white telephone booth with glass panels. The disconnected black telephone inside. The devastation of a people. The rituals of mourning. A language I never learned. Phatic act of enunciating grief. The rotary wheel. The wind at such a height. To carry words or let words be carried away. A giving up—but also: a giving.

●

The point was never the transmission of meaning. The point is only ever to get it down. Or: to let it rise up.

Sarah Carson

No One in This Dumb Bar Will Acknowledge How Famous We Are

Not the girls leaning against the pool table, not the men ignoring their buzzing phones. No one has even stopped by our booth to congratulate you for the time you tackled the 16th ranked running back in the NCAA Division III College Conference of Illinois and Wisconsin. Everyone is pretending they have not read the poem I published in the preeminent literary journal of the central eastern northwestern Great Plains. They've all turned their backs to us, their eyes on the televisions. Ron R. spins the wheel again, and I shout, *I would like to solve the puzzle*. The whole bar erupts. You order another shot. Ten minutes go by. Still no one asks for our autographs. You detail again how you once outran the Baltimore Ravens starting wide receiver before he was the Baltimore Ravens starting wide receiver, and I pretend I have no idea that this story ends with you splayed on the ground, your helmet cracked open like a head gasket. *This is how you love someone*, I tell the waitress on my way to the bathroom, but she does not look up from the notes she's taken about other people's chili cheese fries. When I return, I find her offering you a free Irish car bomb, dropping it into the froth of your Guinness and laughing as you open up your throat like the mouth of a river. She slides into my seat at the table, takes your hand between her fingers. *Finally*, I say to no one, the door to the men's room swinging open. Finally someone who wants the one thing we have.

Anne Champion

Match Girl

It wasn't the rape that ignited me—
my mind has always been a grainy match tip laced
with sulfur: every trespass against my body

struck against it and I blazed rage
until I was soot. My mother's fists,
my father's hands, the boys at school

that snapped my bra, the boys that insisted
my no's meant yes, the girls that called me a slut.
I had to learn survival so I torched

everything I loved before it could ruin me.
I told myself at least the flame was light.
Today I found a video on my computer of my rapist

and I flirting, squeezing lime juice
on our wrists and giving cheers
with a shot glass of tequila, white lines

of cocaine waiting in perfect formation.
I can't be your saint just to receive mercy:
a girl like me knows that truth is always fire.

You think you can rescue me, douse me
in water like a baptism and I'll rise
from my ashes unscorched. You know nothing

about how a girl
can burn and drown
at the same time.

Anne Champion

Why Didn't You Tell Anyone?

After it happened, I started to think
about weird things, like the fact
that humans lived a hundred thousand years
without language.

* * *

I started to think about all the pains I could name.
How do they feel only as nerves pulsing through my body?

* * *

Longing, without the word longing,
is wind whipping through my groin
like a hurricane on a shorefront.
I'm always a little worried
I won't survive it.
I'm always a little worried
that I will.

* * *

Sometimes I'd sit for hours
watching daylight unlace
its hot pink corset, the dark mane
of nightfall draping over me,
and I knew so certainly
there were unevolved things in me
that I haven't found the sound
or typography for.

* * *

It is possible to live a whole life
with a pain lodged in the throat
without the language
to cough it out.

* * *

I tell you,
to look back
is to open your eyes
in salt water
to navigate
your way out
of drowning.

* * *

To find the words
is to sit down
in the eye doctor's chair
and watch blurred truths
suddenly shiver into focus,
better with each lens.

* * *

It's one thing to have words.
And then there's meaning.

* * *

Anne Champion

The placeholder word for all the things we cannot name is God.

* * *

An eclipse is a covering.
An apocalypse is an uncovering.

* * *

Every time I give silence
the body of language
is an inner doomsday.

Sean Cho A.

Waiting on the Next End

The corals are greying   clown fish are wrapping themselves
in dead anemones The redwoods' own proximity causing endless
burn All while you're busy dulling yourself   with self love
I don't blame you   Two weeks ago a farmer unearthed a pterodactyl

wing while uprooting a blood orange tree Now the bones are begging
dust for company in a museum basement   quiet applause   silent
celebration   it wasn't too many lifetimes ago all the prophets
had their tongues ripped out for heeding warnings of this end   I'm trying

to say that all our miracles are mundane and surrounding   topsoil
over clay   a water glass left on your bedside   Don't flatter yourself
if you could time travel back   to preach this ending   you wouldn't
You'd teach all the parrots to recite your name   climb up the clocktower

and proclaim yourself king   or god   Look at you
     apathetic dweller   bewilderment shunner   I'm sorry
Maybe I'm projecting   I want something more powerful
than a god   Please sit down and tell me that story one last time:

the man who got swallowed
up by a blue whale and lived beside krill and shrimp heads
in stomach bile for three days until he tied his undershirt
to the whale's uvula and emerged unharmed   Now

I wake knowing I've been stumbling past my death-place
for years   I wish my father was here
We could dive into the part of the ocean where it's always dark
He'd point out the light hanging above an angler fish's mouth

and I'd pretend it doesn't want us dead

Lisa Compo

A Conjuration for My Daily 4pm Creature

Lately, things have been trapped in a hymn.

    Lately, there's this small heart, humming

against red canna. For some   reason, my body
like a fallen warrior's
        spirit sprung
from a glim   hovers
below a sky that just won't

today. Moisture clings to   screens,
the house sticks   slightly like cooled

cheeks. I keep listening to church
choirs,   I don't believe,   but I don't

feel quite so human
now. Lately, the seasons blend   and I can't remember

when it last felt like a solid   anything. If I had
my own gorget,   I would write

a spell of iridescence
from my throat,   even a knife

couldn't slice me.   What elsc am I
but a battle, a hand,   a voice

in an etude   wringing
scaffolds into wings?   Otherwise, if

I am just this window,

dear warrior visitor, then   you really are
someone's heart

as the Aztecs said.   Someone gone
fighting for this world.   And that is

the enigma begging
to be answered: what transience
                                     have we made, if not already an end?

Britny Cordera

Herbarium

To know the disturbed[1] land better—
like an island in the West Indies that witnessed
the river tamarind as its ruderal species
planted to feed cattle, burn the hair off horses—
a botanist collects as many native plants
as possible and mummifies them in the pockets
of a beat-up school folder. Perfect specimens
with twigs or stems that hold a flower or leaf undamaged,
this kind of life that makes the world want
to get to know them better, make taxonomy
for the green that has no name, moving
slower and smaller than most living things
worth the preservation after all—
like the Jamaican caper overgrown
on the side of a narrow tropical road,
its fragile male and female parts sprawling
forth from a metal barricade meant to keep
the foliage safe from *jeep jeep blue, purple, silver*
driving too far on the left side of the highway.
In her unmarked grave, on an island nearby
a grandmother is vexed at me for following
in her footsteps, walking miles as she did
so I would not have to, on a different path
instead of this road where car horns warn
to keep at bay. Sand blisters and sweat
bluing my feet like a tender Surinam cherry
ready to fall off it's branch when it's purple.
The only thing I want more than to find her
is to know myself in this shared agony;

Forced to walk on this edge where there is no money
or room for a sidewalk, while the caper and everything
else plant-like, (invasive more than native), thrives
in a smog of early morning's rain mixed with diesel
exhaust and heat waves. I wonder, what doesn't want
to be picked this way, to be remembered, then to have
the life pressed out of them.

[1] A term used in Ecology to describe a consequence of human activity on the environment.

Phillip J. Cozzi

The Fabric Anthology of Green

Close your eyes and read with fingertip the fabric anthology of green,
    pledgets bound by Amy, cut from curtain and sweater, napkin and daydress, surgical linen
beginning with the Robin Hood Halloween costume green, the flower stem green,
    the Aunt Norma green, the Indian Ocean, tortoise back, Girl Scout green,

then turn the page to the sun-washed gun-metal green glinting off tanks
    as they ground the rubble of St. Petersburg, Sorrento, Füssen,
moss-drenching viaduct under which you parked your bike and dreamed of Cindy Tonelli,
    avocado of the mind, seeded and sold cold by the bushel on California highways,

green apply jelly bean, bok choy, olive, gallstone, bile, kiwi, jade, the tree weeping like a child,
    the paisley upholstery petrified in Uncle Bruno's living room, verdigris eating Lincoln's profile,
the relief map continent of South America as you palpate the Andes' peaks
    then thumb the threads of Amazon, sycamore veins and the spiky Komodo,

the green-glazed bricks of magic animals in relief on the Temple of Morduk,
    the almost-black green of Rembrandt depicting Aristotle contemplating Homer,
the village of childhood, umbrella pine, Burma, cobalt, ground laurel,
    the clippings of Cubist art on the floor of Ed Toczylowski's Florist Shop,

tongue of glacier blanketing Greenland, as green with envy, nausea, naiveté,
    green encroaching like lichen on log, until all the Earth is green, all is green
as with the phosgene spark which started it all, captured and carried with poles
    and buried with the Ark of the Covenant, with a pot of manna and stone tablets,

to emerge holy in emerald anarchy signifying Spring, as in the first moment
    of the very first season: the green of wild grain at the dawn of human life.

Curtis L. Crisler

Fifty Something Years of ~~Letters~~ Laters
—my paradoxical absolution of Emmett Till

I have two dreams of us. The first, we are sitting
at Navy Pier—lost in the old barges and ships,

when white smog from the mills aren't fogging up
our view. Still, we're in a whiteout of seagulls, diving

for our turkeyburgers and sweet potato fries.
You're telling me about the grandbabies. Miss

Mamie didn't let them run the streets of Chi-town
without her. Everybody they grew up knowing

knew Nana Till's voice too. We met cause a buddy of
mine married a friend of yours. I call breeziness.

The flapping wings of seagulls. The air full of lake
spray and sulfur. This letter starts farther down

the right margin. I don't know, maybe getting older
puts weight on one's shoulders. Funny to say.

You carry us like a mother carries her newborn,
from hospital into this undulating madness, scared

like her frame's full of flames. There are so many of you
and you're only one of you. I am returning to you

like the hawk returns from surveillance, soaring—
not a disturbed flapping of its windblown wings.

It soars, lets the wind uplift it just by breezing.
I am brought back to you, Emmett, 'cause Carolyn

Curtis L. Crisler

Bryant said "Nothing that boy did could ever justify
what happened to him." She only said it fifty-

three-years too late. Some documenter, Tim, got
her to reveal lie she placed in secret locket under

her sternum. With flying birds, the sternum, or
breastplate, is attached to muscles that give to

flight. Carolyn was grounded. She placed lie inside
trinket her heart smothered in. She said nothing

for light years. Your mouth full of snakes, twigs,
and mud. Not a whistle in you. She lived with her

lie like it was the family dog—day in, day out,
until there were no more days for barking.

She outlived giving up her special to a killer she knew
was *the* killer. I can never escape dreaming about

you Em. I wanted to write to you. I'd try being
missive, but I don't know man. I'm shit at

elocution. What's real too, I am shit at avoiding your
probing eyes under that smooth fedora, soliciting

feedback on all that's been going down, up north.
They killing a lot of boys that look like you, Em.

They killing brown women too. They look like your
Mama, Miss Mamie. Sorry for being lax in my

initiative. I'm that new kind of lazy—lost—jaded.
It's probably due to not seeing Miss Mamie

when she came to the church I used to attend in
Fort Wayne. I was too tired. But what's more tired

than death? I had all these questions lined up. What
kind of sparrow or wren flew near her windows that

reminded her of you? Or did she ever move that new
outfit she put out for your return? How long did

it sit on your bed without you in it? I had all these
hugs I gathered from my shelf and put in a bookbag.

Then came the headaches—the second set of dreams.
You smacked against my brain, dislodged pebbles of

rubble-sense I thought I owned. You did so much—
a martyr who didn't know he would matter.

I couldn't tell Miss Mamie about the second set of
dreams. How everyone in them had your face, full

of Tallahatchie River, a bullet, left-over bruises—
the gin fan's barbed wire groove dug deep into

your neck. Their motivation to hold you down in
the silt and grime snapped, got lodged on happenstance.

In these dreams—the deconstruction of your
boyhood—the side-by-side pics of you in killer

fedora, next to you decimated in a coffin—so
panoramic, *this* black and white. *Jet Magazine*—

a subscription to another world. Dreams of your
river face. It was your face on my mother, when she

turned around and said hi. It was your face on
my sisters—coming at me, trying to catch me

as I tried to run away. It was your face on my best friends
faces, throwing your river head to each other. It was your

Curtis L. Crisler

    face on my woman, wailing in gurgles, legs clamping
      me down into all her special. It's weird to be so old

and new—me talking to a fourteen-year-old, when
you're older than me. *What's that?* What can I

    do before my bones become the only information
      all up in me. You are all up in me, like love, is

        what I am struggling to say. I hope you're laughing
          at that. So hard, you shoot milk out your nose.

       I see you in your mother like I see me in my mother.
        I wish they could've met. Man, Carolyn actually

  said, "Nothing that boy did could ever justify what
happened to him." I know. I know. But it seems we just

collecting bodies. A smoking red river full of bodies.
  Yeah, she was scared. But damn. I don't know, Em.

    This sax loving my ears. *This* bass strumming tendrils
      I didn't know I had. *This* drum, my heartbeat.

     It always takes 30, 40, 50 years, if ever, to get
        a justice-slice. *Em? If she would not have lied,*

           it's also possible I would not be thankful.

Jessica Cuello

The Sitters

There was no daycare in those days, she said.

One beat my brother when he peed his pants,
another took us to our father, but our father

didn't live there and we don't know who we saw.

The worst was also our savior, the giant boy
who ran barefoot in the road to pull us from the fire.

He hid the burnt flesh from our eyes, he lay us

on his hard floor while our mother stayed back
with the burning. Once he ripped a mushroom

from my hand that I had saved. I'd cupped it

in my palm but did not press. When I was hungry
I saved my food until I was alone. He flung it past

the fence. *This is poison.* After the fire I don't remember

where we slept or what we wore. One time I stared
from the sidewalk while his mother gripped his neck.

With the other hand she shoved a bar of soap into

his mouth again, again. It didn't fit and I watched
in silence because that's what we did with pain.

Leia Darwish

Notes (In Retrograde)

A mobile that hangs from the ear.
I remember not to sign any contracts.
Amnesia for the rest.
What you are afraid of
packed away in mourning.
Chlorine, the water in wood:
I smell it at the bottom of an exhale.
I'm not alone in this body.

Elisabeth Reidy Denison

The Student Considers the Hyacinth Girl

The tutor says: "It's about sidestepping an experience, in this case erotic, amid a more general air of un-fulfillment." Spring is the student's most embarrassing time of year. She insists on communicating. She pursues clarification, to her cost.

She speaks in class: "Sure, but it's an eroticism of the mind." And the tutor: "Isn't all eroticism inherently mental?"

She means it's protraction, depicted. The protraction of a single possibility, possibility sustained to breaking point, to the threshold of abstraction. The class proceeds to discuss ways of falling short—thwarting of instinct, lapses of nerve—

to which the student adds: "The facts of the moment (the arms spilling with offering, the hair damp) are still intact here. There is an instant of overlap between what exists and what is coming apart. At least until the next lines, when all at once the girl's eyes are going and her words are going and…"

It seems her sleeve snags on the moment at the time, then again on the memory of it. Each subsequent recollection is another tug to eventually free the sleeve.

To close the hour, the tutor delivers a brief commentary on the overwrought likening of blooming to obscenity. The student looks outside, where a clutch of daffodils are really taking it from the wind.

She thinks: *In spring I always have to be told.*

Brandon Thomas DiSabatino

"open all night"

a clinical wind folds
the sumac back

officers fall asleep
in their squad cars

grassblades bend from
the boots of young boys

(dragging the lakes
for their brothers)

their flashlights move
like rosicrucians in the fog

Aline Dolinh

Still Life with Beheaded Chicken

I don't want to believe how easy it is. To brace myself for the killing, I think about those sexy, gleaming Dutch genre paintings—the ones where the flimsy wooden tables are always so garish with meat. I position myself as the austere milkmaid, utterly blinded by my halo of braids. Somebody hands me a knife and my palm opens like a hidden message on the keening edge. The people are impatient. I strike out only knowing that I must hurt something with competence. I am not sure what softness I will abolish. I listen for the squawk, brace my red-wet hands for writhing. But I only feel the moment as the throat slackens. The once-white feathers wilt fast and I am surprised by how marvelously my hands can take something away. It's beautiful in the same way it feels beautiful to crack an egg perfectly in one go, not even a slip of shell drowning in the bowl—just that sopping golden eye gazing up at me in all its pride.

Lara Egger

How to Operate Under Normal Conditions

Things get rabbit. Things get rabbit really fast.
The sky is on repeat; there are never enough
blue crayons. Sometimes meaning
gets in the way of understanding. As in opera,
for example, or the Ten Commandments.
In a parallel universe I am God's favorite
imaginary friend. In a parallel universe, I'm intrepidly
polyamorous. After it rained, we all agreed the air
smelled like something familiar. Am I being familiar?
My mother says all this preemptive grief
is ruining my skin. That scene in the movie
where the lover runs through the airport
to stop the other lover from getting on the plane
might be cliché but it doesn't make that kind of certainty
less enviable. Shake 'N Bake fireworks.
Bathroom fandango. I'm up for anything
as long as it's liaison-forward.
When the problem is solved we go back to our desks
and invent another one. There isn't any trick
to sword-swallowing. Just don't swallow.

Michael Frazier

The Japanese Characters for Kindness are 親切 Meaning *Parent* and *Cut*

If I wasn't cut   out of my mother   she would have bled out
Mother   my first cry   mother cut   out of the picture

Still a mama's boy   my folks doubt

if I'll ever get married   I know it's a kindness   when a child leaves the nest
But it's also a kindness   when a mother says *Don't go*

& her boy brings his head to her chest

Between Housewives of Atlanta gifs   and selfies in her Minnie Mouse onesie:
John Gray YouTube sermons   and reminders to *Put on the armor*

before leaving the house   She says, *Rely less on me*

& more on God   But wasn't it a woman   who gave the gospel
legs? I know what they say   about boys like me   But will you check on her

if it's been more than 48 hours?   Will you leave poems   or verses of the Bible

in her voicemail?   Will you listen   to her complain   about some busted guy
who tried it, or deer   on her commute?   *If you love someone, let them go.*

Why?

Michael Frazier

Irrational Fear of Home

        There are many ways to be called back home: the nose
dive of a plane, the punctuation of a pistol, my bike

                folded into a red crane gazing up at God. I think I love
this world too much. Gifted with wide nostrils, I inhale

                      &tighten like a balloon ready for flight
or for bursting. I know

                        what they say: eight glasses of water, eight hours of sleep;
I eat less meat, but fail going vegan after a week. Alone,

                      I watch a crane crash into the black
churning river. Dusk spreads like a rash. A mosquito

                            ripens on my bicep. In its bulging abdomen
                   I swirl outside myself: here & not here. What I give

                    I take back with the smack
of my palm. What makes me desirable?

        My always summer
skin? Why do they want my blood?

    Am I really as sweet
as swinging fruit?

⌂   ⌂   ⌂

        If you're lucky
you spend most of your life asleep. Your mind

                loosened like baby teeth. Kids don't question
       Tooth Fairy logic: bone

               returned, re-fleshed, with a face. I tied
      my canine to the doorknob,

               slammed. Crooked-toothed gape of the man
      who slams the brakes on the bus & today

               is not the day I return home
      to my mother as a pension payment. I walk

               to school shaking like a tambourine
          on a restless knee. I remember the caved-in helmet.

        The exhaust pipe burning calf to bone. The fence blown
     into my sternum. My fragility makes me

    a man. My mother
says, *don't come home*

   to America, because it's safer in Japan: no guns
or police who will follow me

like history. I can run
from a bullet, like my father, but

what if I can't run

Michael Frazier

from myself? Fear can make a home

        out of a body. Nowhere on this earth is heaven
if there's no peace within me.

                ⌂   ⌂   ⌂

        Who isn't negotiating
with death? Who isn't searching for a god? I've been saying, *I need*

           to get my life right before He comes back
since Sunday School. Right now

               in a lilied muumuu, my grandmother sits
where she's sat for thirty years. One hand

                   rubbing a knee. Another clutching
her landline. Humming

                        Juanita Bynum. Waiting
for heaven

                          to pick up. She knows something
I don't. A sickle of moon

                  light invades my room. Can't close my eyes
until I pray: One day a third of the sun will darken.

        The moon will turn to blood. The stars shot from the sky.
I'll be given a white stone with my new name.

        I'll have no memory of my old home.
            I'll be unkillable

      forever
   amen.

Elizabeth Galoozis

Black and White

Your lab partner leans down,
listening for some crackle or
hum from your just-constructed battery.
Chalk dust pervades the space.
The black table is ringed in white
from past experiments. Your hand is just
centimeters from hers. This frame
captures one September in
a series: it is always time
to learn about electricity.
Here, everyone is always eleven.
They're always seconds away
from a new understanding,
from learning the intended
lesson, or some other unpleasant
or exciting thing, winding into
the brain like a wire, recurring knowledge
vibrating inopportunely:
your dead father. This girl your mother
objects to on sight. The principles
of power. How many minutes remain
in the hour.

Adam Gianforcaro

Fever Dream as Cardio

First I am dream with gym shorts
under sweatpants. Then I am dream
with crowbar. That is, I wake

in the locker room to the sound of faggot
on a straight man's tongue. I dream
of turning the tides, dream it into being.

Is it just me or does the word *pry*
sound incomplete? & yet body parts leak
& swell. Think of this leaking, this swelling,

as anything but phallic. Think brains instead.
Think the sound of a can opening, the smell
of ground meat in a gym bag. I keep going.

Act two has me heading for the elliptical. I see
the man with tongue behind me in wall mirrors.
My pores pump shrapnel. My skin itches. Somewhere

behind me: a monologue, a discovery.
I consider logistics. A nontarget's privilege.
The prophecies of passing. When I dream

I am always dream with crowbar. A lust
for bones experimenting with role play.
I have always had a thing for curtains parting.

Jessica Goodfellow

Lumen

A lumen is a measure of light over time,
a unit of luminous flux, weighted
for the vagaries of the human eye
This means: no humans, no lumens—
though still there could be light.

Poor lumens. We are reckoning
a wreck, and taking them with us,
who never did anything but radiate
in all directions from a source of light.

We are taking with us mile markers,
marzipan and every canvas
that has ever been stretched over a frame.
We are taking with us commas, and blue-
prints, and prayer. We are taking
Venn diagrams, and suicide, and suede.

Sea shanties, pixels, and regret:
when I was eleven, sitting in the back
of my parents' van, hot wind on my face
as I watched the wheat fields go by,
I sometimes saw the farmer, his face
embroidered with what I now know
was drink. We are taking with us
that memory, and the revision

Jessica Goodfellow

of that memory. Equations, weather-
vanes, and puns. Symphonies, all of them.
We are taking with us yoga, and genocide,
the alphabet and shame. We are taking irony
and velvet and taxes. We are taking with us
haiku, and treaties, and the breaking of treaties.
Graph paper, sonnets, and dread: tuck them in
our pockets—here we go—human,
a unit of evolutionary flux. And when we are
gone, still there will be light.

Hayley Graffunder

Doomsday Baby & I

are used to the bombs.
We have our routine when they detonate
at 3 am. She doesn't cry, just looks at me
like we might as well eat, since we're up.
There's no shrapnel; it's not bad. The air
is as warm as we want it to be.
Doomsday Baby ages forward & back
each night. Sometimes, she is three years old,
squeezing the ends of my fingers
as we sneak around a post-apocalyptic
underground complex. We risk it all
on the hope of a hidden school—
even in the end, my baby will learn to read.
Other times, she is an infant wrapped
to my chest as we roam dusty streets,
silent besides the thrum of her little heart,
the only bird-like thing left on earth.
The beginning remains fuzzy, though
we go back often. When we do,
Doom swells my abdomen with her doll-like
limbs. News stations report on killer wasps,
ballistic threats, nukes & famine,
but she hums beneath my skin
a song about wildflowers.
I give birth in an empty hospital,
think *of course, this is how I got her* as I clutch
her to me for the hundredth time.
Some nights Doom doesn't visit.
I sit at attention, ready to comb her hair
until I droop on the bed, still dressed,
dreaming of other babies. Having grown

Hayley Graffunder

unwilling to live in a world of rosebuds
with no Doom, I pray over soft hairs
webbed in the comb—that the sun won't rise,
that the earth will split open
& suck every living thing through its teeth
so I know she will always return to me.

Hayley Graffunder

Doom & the Elephant in the Room

Today, Doom turns four years old.
Her hair is still blonde, & she hasn't perfected
the word *strawberry*, as she's never tasted one.
She is the oldest she has ever been—
& I am too—but the truth is she is eternal:
when my sweet Doom waters our plant,
she says she can feel it growing, touches the stem
where, the next day, two leaves will sprout.
Such knowing warms the room, demystifies
our survival; maybe we are alive because she is.
After sunset, she climbs onto my lap
with her favorite book, my grandfather's
old guide to flora. It's cruel to show her
what she's missing, what I killed to get her,
but I open it anyway, to the hostas,
then the elephant ears, their black & white
illustrations. I describe how my mother
tended them, how each year on my birthday
the leaves were bigger than my head.
Now, I have four gray hairs growing
along the crown. I lower my head for Doom
to see them shine silver in the candlelight.
She combs through & asks *were hostas gray, too?*
I shake my head: *Gray hair happens when people
get old. Hostas stayed green forever*, I tell her.
Now let's blow out your birthday candle. She knows
already that candles once topped cakes.
I hold a taper we use to see after dusk,
tell her to take her time, to make as many
wishes as she wants. She exhales immediately,
in a rush, tells me she only had one.

Benjamin S. Grossberg

Imaginary Litter Boxes with Real Cats in Them

Despite my insistence to the contrary, he is alive.
His presence soils social media. Little pyramids
of tacks left behind each of my tires.
Despite my insistence, the guy who lurched

into midlife face, the one suddenly
jowly, sallow, sweating in a pink polo, that
wasn't him. Maybe it was me. When asked
if she'd be married to the President if he weren't

rich, she said, *If I weren't beautiful, do you think he'd—*
then tossed her head a little, her hair
shimmering like a curtain of energy.
Despite my insistence, the man in question

couldn't love me. I'd put my foot down, pointed
at his trainers and the tracks across the linoleum.
Lifted the mop and sloshed it into the bucket
as punctuation. Last year, a Russian boy died

when melted permafrost exposed the carcass
of a reindeer, animating the anthrax
of a previous century. From the point of view
of the anthrax, this is a story not unlike

"Sleeping Beauty." While he and I were making
love, as we sometimes did, deep into the afternoon,
permafrost was melting. On social media,
he is looking for other men. Other *men*. That's

what he said. I dreamed that a god spoke
from the mouth of an ant and the sun darkened.
This was not a frightening dream, though
clearly the apocalyptic plays out individually

as well as collectively. Like fascism does. And
biosphere collapse. They advertise *budget
travel to destinations your mother would rather you—*.
Perhaps in our moment, poetry can only aspire

to the irony of current events. Despite his
insistence, it is a man, singular, one man, he is
looking for. A different one. Leaving his house,
I mean that last time, it seemed I tripped

as into an ice-melt fissure, a moulin boring
miles deep into a glacier, its melt water
pure neon blue. My hands flew up
in front of me as I fell. Due to wind resistance,

I couldn't lower them back to my sides.
I did my best to keep my eyes open.

Kathleen Hellen

On white appearance of a wall
After "Evening Snow at Kanbara"

you believe in the solidity of things:
houses shuttered against storm. The pines
encumbered, rooftops laden, stooped
figures trudging up the slope through snow
falling thick: hallucination—
the snow—even lightly—rarely falling
on the station at Tōkaidō Road
that connects Kyōto
with the capital at Edo

—even as the footprints follow yellow
hat, leggings beni pink—even as your foot
is sinking in the drift on thinnest paper, glistening
with expectation through shades of cinder, Prussian blue

Ambalila Hemsell

Fire Season

The calla lily is a meditation on doom.
The design so clean, the pollen so yellow.
I count seven chickadee shadows. They stretch
and bounce over the dead lawn, the blooming tangelo
poppies. It is windy in the garden. The wind as restless
as a river. My love, we have lost so much of this year.
I alone swallowed several months, you hid
others in your pockets, balled up and forgotten.
I find myself inside a Gilbert box. There are some birds,
a lover, and some fruit. There are neat limits
to what the box can hold. Inside the box, the poppies
are indifferent to the drought and you, a sailboat, borrow
their grace. The months wash up on shore, broken.
Bearded irises break open and hang their petals
down like tongues. Coral and butter, an embarrassment
of symbolism. There is no box, of course, but somehow all of this
is held together anyway.

Maura High

Still Life

I look at myself through the rainy window.
The water in the jam jar stains the air,

and the scene I am painting at the kitchen table

blurs and scumbles. I lean closer,
but can't make out the subject:

the ringed milk jug and an apple? Spools

of varicolored thread, the dress-making scissors?
My grandmother in her apron of scraps glides

from door to fireplace and curtsies,

a shimmer of purposefulness.
I rap the pane and the drops slither

to the sill and pool there. The rain

slicks my hair and trickles down my neck,
patters on the glass roof of the lean-to,

the slate roof of the coal shed.

She rises and floats between the me at the table
and me at the window: bright, dark, bright.

Excell N. Hunter

Sobbing Sky
I See You

Get to the tiny bathroom window
in the middle of New Orleans
stand tiptoe on the Saint Bernard Project tub
tipped across onto sharp ashy elbows
I begin the life now begin the night begin
the accounting. Did I say it's pouring?
Did I say I am poor and boy again?

The storm coils leaking about itself
callous restive white python of people
and explodes electric sulfite with drums
that can watch out hurt your ears.
Unmanned fire hose winds demanding this
of others by its issue there let go
slapping away with the offered hand
dumping on trees flowers roads rocking houses
pushing on in giant biblical sheets
each long hymn of waters wrath-like.
You see its silver shower challenge? Yes,
in one metallic tasting drop at a time
on the tongue. Just say lip. And coin.

Sobbing sky I see you. I recognize your
chilly living ozone gusts
inhaled sparkler flashes
eyes opened big suspicious expectant
noted how a cloud-swelled ceiling
at will can frighten any day.

Excell N. Hunter

Marbles of water made it in one at a time
a tear of a red cent dime a nickel two bits
plunk the sound of each to an empty head.
I assay then accept each. I accept each.
A parent of all my senses and delights
gave me a first piece to compare
another storm ago. Plunk.

In the hurried dream old age
the beckoning of water rests pauses from challenge
gives time for a little thing to be drawn
let it in to what I since had populated
pawned polluted. I sense the rain's intent
gaze into its eyes so many lights touch fingers to lips and
define a small moral.

Korey Hurni

On the Pacific Coast Highway

Jeremiah is too sure of himself after playing with cadavers all morning. *Set aside all natural attitudes and, well, the world opens up*, his ballroom eyes filling with late afternoon light, *at least that's how I see things*. He complains for an hour about forgetting his sunglasses while driving on the PCH. I wanted to know how a scalpel felt in capable hands, if it felt, after time, like an extension of yourself. When you know something so well you step beyond the self, reaching with certainty. Like the waist we sleep against, the one our hand fumbles for without thinking, and how awfully soft it feels when it isn't there.

I wanted to know if the scalpel helped remind him of his body. *You learn to stop noticing it*, he said and I too grew annoyed by all of California's light. How it made the world appear wide and inviting, and how easy it was to misjudge distance and how beautiful the cliff beaches really are with all their sea rats. How clear it is to see the truck driver notice the dog, but only soon enough to stop on top of it. We all hear the bones breaking. I wonder if the driver, who I imagine must feel the truck as an extension of himself, if he can feel them snapping and snapping like a migraine. The brakes do nothing but tie the dog up in the tires. Jeremiah says it would have been better if the driver just sped up. *It's quicker*, he stresses, *it would have finished the job.*

Instead there is a bright howling as though it were suddenly morning and the sun bleeds through what you thought was a thick enough curtain. How you feel it all run through you until it goes silent. Your hand pats the bed and then it seems louder.

Adeeko Ibukun

Night Cabaret

The doors mean/ there is a passage even in the night/
the passage means/ we can leave and leave behind
a story/ a story means/ someone is guilty/ under the shelf
a dark box rattles again and again with its wandering rats/
it means/ there are animals trying to find their paths in the night/
o'/ it'd be/ all of us trying to find our paths in the night/ I
mean/ there is a weight everyone carries through the world
as an inheritance/ o'/ does it mean/ it is needless to say needs
wheel through needs and the doors are no more/ or to say/
teach me how to hold on to the balance before falling/
the world means/ I am rolling on with my mother's mirror
and it's with its scampering animals/ it means/ the scuttling/
the howling/ the hunt/ the world means/ it is all we've learnt
of all our animals in the tilt of our balance/ it is/ the people/
the governments/ the wars/ the doors also mean/ we can
wait and wait behind for all the surprises/ my mother comes in
in the slither of the life/ she is/ the warm slice of the dance
in the give of the hours/ the doors mean/ there is a passage
even in the night/ I sing and mean/ I am my mother in my
mother's mirror/ it means/ how heavier and heavier I have
become/ losing my innocence to the dark/ the world then
means/ I am making more rooms for all our animals/
my mother sings with me/ here is my darkness/ take yours

Rebecca Irene

Insufficient

All I wanted was a twenty
from the ATM—the comfort
whir of a Jackson for gas,
parking, & a smoothie.
Instead, green blinking
pixels—*insufficient funds*.
Then, a paper receipt. Insufficient:
inadequate:unable:lacking:broken:
askew:damaged:can't make
the grade:less than:deficient:
cracked. I walk to work, go
without, try to shrug it off.
Clients over-tip
because I'm old
& still waiting
tables. Smile.
We all know how this works—
specials, orders, we give you
what you want. Mid-shift,
the word stops
plaguing me.
The ways we learn
to cope, make do.
Ask me.

Nazifa Islam

Fortunes

a found poem: Virginia Woolf's
The Waves

I am not beautiful, but I have never stopped
undressing like I am

summer heat or the storm-tinted scent of herbs.
I carry passion in my pinkish hands.

I follow love
and happiness to their red gate.

I like the cold smell of wet leaves on the ground
and the teething ferocity of the sea.

I like to see children dance
in fields—their nails bitten, their eyes content.

But more than anything—
more than laughter—I like to walk

through the long beautiful seasons
clutching at time

like it will let me be
old one day.

Kenneth Jakubas

Letter Constructing a Face

— For My Missing Grandfather

Anyone who stages their death becomes you, inventor of the disappearing man. How long you been in love with air? Is it that much in your hair? In the backyard of the woman you disappeared from is a garden the size of your prison cell— you are not a wanted ghost. You're there dwelling in a periscope high on the shelf *we don't touch*. What happened to your happening? There are plots in the image of a mask I've drafted of your American seizure. A lightning bolt, mortar. Tonight I look at the black oval around this waning crescent moon, and I think, not-precisely, of my existence. There's your margin. Even the wind, I know, competes with the freedom I have of constructing your face. You could have held us together like birds even, making life in their thimble mouths. In my land of freedom, my mother hates you in the spirit of the unfinished wars; my body burns you a letter from this desert about a daughter who gave birth to a little boy in a forest of disbelief.

Susan Johnson

And I Ask You America

Was the shooter an angry white guy with easy access to guns? Was the shooter an angry white guy with easy access to guns? Was the shooter an angry white guy with easy access to guns? Was the shooter an angry white guy with easy access to guns? Was the shooter an angry white guy with easy access to guns? Was the shooter an angry white guy with easy access to guns? Was the shooter an angry white guy with easy access to guns? Was the shooter an angry white guy with easy access to guns? Was the shooter an angry white guy with easy access to guns? Was the shooter an angry white guy with easy access to guns? Was the shooter an angry white guy with easy access to guns? Was the shooter an angry white guy with easy access to guns? Was the shooter an angry white guy with easy access to guns?

Michal "MJ" Jones

"I Always Wanted to Bang A Black Boi"

Another high bright stage and I'm on it.
White girl here has written me a sonnet.
Wants to wear me as a shoe, try out my
soul to season pale flesh. My skin reason
enough or kin enough to fin her tongue
across its ash. *Do I detect a hint*
of grits? Dashes of cornmeal? Paprika?
Rum? What is it? What is it? What are you?
She sees no monkeys here. They're on her back,
whip shit at my evasive slip. I dip.
Lightened to live long enough for questions.
Go where I know she's not to follow, no.

In sky void of stars. Moon eludes its bright.
She will not embrace this curtain of night.

Aseem Kaul

Clearing the air

because I am guilty
you must interrogate my silence

I understand you perfectly
and I confess
the way the river swallows a cast stone

for your convenience
I am no longer allowed to use in your presence
words like justice or freedom
you may confiscate these if you like

I shall declare truthfully my intentions
for you to inspect
when you search me

of nothing but your ignorance
till it confirms what you assume

dear tyrant
I have swallowed your insults
its waters rising imperceptibly

I have packed a suitcase of words
not even in my own tongue
or home
now that dialog is contraband

and empty the deep pockets of my memories
but beware, this poem is a sharpened object
it may stick.

Rogan Kelly

Your Jazz Mouth All Over Monday Morning

On Wythe, near 5th, outside *The 12 Chair Cafe*, a Lyft pulls next to an Uber, blocks the thruway. I post sentry over luggage while you divine for coffee. One fare bound for Penn. The other for JFK. The drivers commune in the street while the traffic runs idle. It's nearly Thanksgiving and the holdup is making me sweat. One driver says to the other, *hey which way to the bridge?* The other points a crooked finger at the pink starling arch that crowns the back of his head. You beeline for me. *Must be love*, the one driver shouts over the trumpeted horns. *Fuck \ nobody \ I mean \ never \ loved me like that * the other pines. You make the ground pound the sky with your mouth on my mouth. You make the backed-up-street-chorus go hush in the wake of your wow! Your bright body is a speakeasy cabaret. I don't notice the hot cup you put in my hands.

David Keplinger

Birthday

The farthest star we can see is five billion light years from my hometown, somewhere east of the city of Reading. After school our mother took us to Reading to buy our coats, already winter, fifty years ago. It was always on my birthday. The star is called *Icarus* and can only be seen because it is magnified by bent space, as if by old glass in one of the old farmhouses. My birthday came and went with a thick fur hood and a padded coat, that's for certain, but now I remember so little of that time, the effort and the money crumpled in her purse, the feeling she must have had of drowning, how she hated the cold, the wind, how Reading on the icy roads, driving there and back at night, seemed farther and farther away.

Chris Ketchum

Powerline

On our walk, you told me about a man I hadn't heard of.
He'd sent you a picture of his runner's footprints,
a trail postholed in the twilight-blue snow.

You said it was nothing—mostly emails. A visit
in Portland, Denver, then New York.
The wind faltered as we turned into the park,

vacant and cold in the early autumn night.
At the playground's edge, an oak had been cleaved
in two by the afternoon storm, its heartwood burning

under the moonlight like a pale and solitary flame.
Broken limbs lined up against the curb
like they were waiting to be taken, a powerline

tangled in the branches. The wire twisted
over asphalt, and through the wet black grass
glistening with streetlight.

A segment of it hung across the slide's pink chute—
the last few feet that flatten out, to deliver a kid
softly down to the woodchips, enlivened and wild,

wet-assed from the pool of raindrops. We stopped.
I leaned an ear to the cable, careful not to touch,
but it didn't sizzle or hum. It just kind of lay there,

like a body emptied of its purpose, a symbol
from a language neither of us spoke. I wondered
if we should call someone. You thought it best

Chris Ketchum

to leave it there—whoever's job it was to come
would come. You said he must be on his way,
or would be, or it didn't matter at all.

Ashley Sojin Kim

Last Frost

Autumn signaled harvest time, the coolness
of white and pale-green roots, plump and waiting
to be pulled up from the ground. The radishes
were fond of Soo, whose old but able hands
prepared them as her mother had: small plates
of kimchi cubes and pickled yellow moons
or thin, translucent squares in bone-broth soup.
They almost lasted through the winter, giving
comfort where they could. The river grew
a skin of ice while Soo poured molten syrup
onto clean snow and ate the stars she drew,
delicate and short-lived like the daylight.
In March, the field began to breathe and thaw
and covered Soo with fresh hibiscus blooms.

Kathleen Kirk

Death of a Sasquatch

Attention must be paid, said his wife,
writing to the scientists.

It's possible to die from lack of recognition,
she went on, convinced,

                     but day after day
he sat lumpish on the lip of the crater

until he went down to the basement
of his mind, where he did not exist.

emilie kneifel

Dreaming

little tumbles awake. his voice for once is a warble. i had a twin he says. a twin. but every time i tried to touch her she wedged. i hold his forehead to his ears. i close his eyes with my ribbon. i'm alone he shivers so i curl on his chest and i hum. i tell him the longest story i know. then big landed on your nose and you sneezed, remember, and i was a turtle when you gave me my shadow—i tell him all of our lives, all of our lives until it becomes a narration. until his shivers brittle and skitter away.

Susanna Lang

Poste Restante

Dear swallows,

The homes you excavated in the sandy bank
remain, perfect rounds of shadow. No intruders
will come inside while you're away, not light,
not blackbirds that harried your nestlings—at most
a little snow. The air misses your conversation,
your swinging arcs. You embarked so early,
before it seemed time to make my preparations.
I am left unready for all that is to come.

Dear asters,

You will leave too, though you are everywhere
I go now, clouds of blue and magenta
along the paths. Now that the bees have found you
their honey must taste of stars.
Butterflies cloak you in their wings,
they will steer their journeys by your light.
But I am not fooled, or only a little
during these last warm days. It will not be long.

Dear postmaster,

I do not know how or when the recipients
will retrieve these postcards—they are traveling
with no fixed itinerary. I hope you will not
allow the cards to be lost, or send them

to the dead letter office. If you retire, please
leave a note for your successor. The travelers
have no sense of time or geography.
I do not know if they can even read the words.

Dear ventricle,

It is hard to keep a beat when you are so tired.
Sometimes you have to pause, take a break
despite the outsized consequences, race to catch up
as the world spins around you. Once you held
the band together, steadiness your greatest virtue,
with the occasional flashbang of a solo. You played
the standards with your own flair. Now you stumble
as you leave the stage, catch yourself on the rail.

Dear bats,

I only saw you once or twice this season and now
it is too late—you will not take your crooked flight
above our maple, not this year and I can no longer
promise myself you'll return in the hour between
light and dark when the evenings grow long again.
We do not understand why your colonies are dying
but we know they are. Soon the children will pull on
bat masks and their ritual cries will be all we have left.

Dear liberty,

Susanna Lang

You must know how this will end, even as you pull
a gas mask over your head and step out the door,
armed with an umbrella and the makings of fire.
You have walked these streets, or parallel streets
in distant cities, these last months and many years ago.
Always that lone figure, arm raised in a heroic gesture,
points the way. Always an army, and the dead heaped
on the paving stones, smoke billowing overhead.

Dear rooster,

You have been practicing, and your voice has grown
in power and timbre, ringing out from the henhouse next door
as I make breakfast. Fortunate for you that I wake up
with the thump of the paper against the door, the sky still dark
these chilly mornings. In France, a cock named Maurice
won a court case and kept his life though the neighbors
complained. But you are likely to be soup before long—
a small tragedy as tragedies go these days, but still a loss.

Dear spirits,

I hear you less and less—so many others clamor
to be heard. What can you still need to say to me?
The stories you did not find time to tell before
will remain untold: even you have forgotten them.
The ones I already know, I've told again and again.
There are no words for what remains: this small
stillness at the core of me, quiet pool where dragonflies
skim the surface and grasses dip to meet the water.

Scot Langland

Triolet Grief

at 17

He lips along my stubble line.
our buttons slip; my hips sashay
as if the perfume's mine.
He lips along my stubble line;
his fingers stray down thighs aligned.
I think you're gay, he seems to say
as he lips along my stubble line.
Our buttons slip; my hips sashay,

and like a man, he's satisfied.
He brushes my whispered questions off,
letting our clothes fall down in stride.
Like a man, he's satisfied
for now—at least I tried.
Leaving me here, he scoffs
at my uncertainty. He's satisfied.
He brushes my whispered questions off.

at 25

Your golden iris swells. You're through,
    and in a photograph
        you're just a slight of light I never knew.
Your golden iris tears on through,
        revealing sleights I never knew
        you took. Like an epitaph,
        your golden iris swears we're through.
But in a photograph

Scot Langland

your golden flecks in green break me
        apart like pollen dusting leaves.
        Late summer buzzing down from trees,
your golden flecks in green break me
        in twos and threes as if we're all degrees
        of light perceived. Please leave
        your golden flecks in green; break me
apart like pollen dusting leaves.

Our imitation dream devolves
        in darkroom trays. Your eyes deflect
        in waves of golden hair cascades.
Our imitation dream devolves
        in waves of golden hair cascades.
        Underexposed, unwashed,
        our imitation dream devolves
in darkroom trays. Your eyes deflect.

at 33 ½

I brush familiar hues across
my face in lines of sky-lit blue,
and next I'll tint my cheeks with moss.
I brush the thinning hues across
        my cheek,
            freckled and tensed
with suffixes of you:
            the man transferred.
I branch the thinning hues across
my face:
        a scene deferred

to all but you. I want to dye
my mind with glints of lust,
a young man's shade.
            Nearby,
rain streaks the ground, and trees supply

my audience,
replacing you. But you still dye
my mind
         in shades of lust.

In the bathroom, I am mirrored, canvassed,
stretched tight against a bone-bare frame,

beholden to my disgust. Fractious

in the bathroom, I practice
hollowing
         my cheeks with blush.

Outside, I'm colorless, renamed

disgust:
      a canvas botched,
      a face reframed,
stretched tight
      in paint-chipped shame.

For years, transformed, I loved the night,
but now,
         through a window, a bone-bare tree
shadows my bed with limbs, and I see
my lines; my arms stretch out in the night.
Through a window, a bone-bare tree
         branches the bed we bought,
           and I'm left my inconsistencies,
             my back-and-forths,
               my in-betweens,
and with these blurring hues,
I loose
    myself
        as if this need belongs to someone else.

Scot Langland

at 12

He stretches out across white sheets.
His painted lips leave streaks
in bed like winding streets.
He stretches out against white sheets
to wrinkle Mother's pleats.
She cinches curtain-light across his cheeks.
He stretches out across white sheets.
His painted lips leave streaks.

Mariana Lin

One Night in Melchior Islands

You almost died.
I, your neighbor, sharing a padded wall,
was lying still,
waiting for my mind
to spill over the icy floe,
the marled ocean silk.
I wanted to dream—
there was so much water—
but instead I heard a howling,
bellied, dizzy,
a beast scrabbling for the moon.
It was your voice
unready to die,
gutting the air for sugar—
gutting your blank body for a sign.
I called for help, the doctor came,
fed you the sweetness of gleaming oranges, white rolls, crackers, red veined honey,
whatever they've loaded this ship with so we all don't die.
But we're still alone, you and I,
nudging onwards
through the cold untrampled islands,
split like sliced bellies,
fish full of ice.
This ship full of papery lives.
What is there left to scream for?
You,
tender stranger in lilac,
your white head, a moon, an eye—

Christopher Locke

Counting

My daughter Grace has a weakness
for crows, points to one hopping the lid
of the café dumpster, its shoulders oiled
black as Elvis' pomp. And when we drive
home, two crows tightrope the highway's
yellow line, tap a squirrel pressed dry
as a flower. Even as I speed past they
are fearless, pompous struts like federal
judges before they sentence you to life.
I will release my crows on an unsuspecting
world and they will do my bidding, Grace
says. And I laugh, imagine a wide cape
of darkening sky as they fan out behind
her in a staccato of barks and cries. Home,
the car ticks in the driveway as I stand
in the yard, spy three adjourned in a sugar
maple: silent, disapproving, their languorous
stares unsure if they've noticed my face before.
Grace startles me from behind, places a silver
necklace in my hand. Leave it on the stump,
she says, so they'll know it's theirs. And
when I look back up, there are now four.

Anthony Thomas Lombardi

upon hearing Prince sing "Purple Rain" at First Avenue in Minneapolis in 1983, I begin to understand my mother's love life

I don't want your money, no no no no
I don't even think I want your love—
    — Prince Rogers Nelson

I confess. my sorrow will eat more
of me than any kind of hunger.

I steam up phone booths with tears,
I overdress for my own funeral.

my eager heart is my mother's
eager heart.

heaven is darker than I was led to
believe, so I take light

where I can: my throat bright
with amethysts, the kitchen's dim glow

like a searchlight in a prison yard.

my mother loves most what enables her
to be lonely.

Anthony Thomas Lombardi

the ashtray is glutted with hours,
the car won't even start anymore,

but I know times are changing.
new wind brushes the jasmines,

their bloom leans away from me.
the moon waxes & wanes.

I hate to see anything so lovely   alone.

Tara Mesalik MacMahon

Did You Know Paradise Means

walled garden? I wanted to be a boy. The strum
of Papa, spit of fire, finger-comb hair-back cool.
        And August flesh, dark as dirt and clouds—
                those muscular clouds I don't know yet.

Hand-blown glass-pitchers, full—
from the fall-down bright lemons.
        But the Iced-Tea-King, my twin,
                the lost fraternal
to the Empress of Ice-Cream—would he know?—
                      the magic hip-hop of lemons
                          in a shade like that?

        Like *thiz*,
      like that.
         Aunt Z talks like *thiz*.
                Throws salt, chews dip—
    and juzt cuz a gator'z got
zealed-lidz,

      don't mean he zleepz.
          She dabs *cook-zoda*

                  on my *zwamp-kneez*.

      How to find, how to find?—
      zwag pure gold
              for any fool?—

            the brother I don't know yet know.

Angie Macri

Elegy

In the water, a serious reflection:
her face drawn into sky
without clear features,
as if eyes, nose, mouth, mean nothing
even after all that practice.
An infant thinks it a game
to learn those words, and adults
say no different. But here the child
finds herself a blur. The pasture
waves around her, once prairie,
now barbed wire between the house
and this stockpond, an eye
men cut with a backhoe
so the cattle would never go thirsty.
Laundry whips on the clothesline
as two halves of bodies drying
again and again in her and her parents'
sizes. She touches her face.
It seems the pieces are still,
but the water says never.
A red-tailed hawk circles,
followed by flame.

Elizabeth Majerus

If You Are a White Person

If you are a white person at a protest, one of the most helpful things you can do is to stop other white people from destroying things, and publicly identify them if possible. The white people destroying things are *not* there to help.
   —@DavidOAtkins, 5/30/2020

One of the most helpful things you can do
is to stop other white people
from destroying things.
Publicly identify them if possible.

The white people destroying things are *not* there to help.

One of the things you can do is most helpful if possible
to stop other publicly destroying white people
from things. Identify them.

The white people destroying things are *not* there to help.

If you a white person are there to help,
one of the most helpful things you can do is protest to stop
other white people from destroying things,
and identify a possible at them publicly.
The white people are *not* not destroying things.

If you are a white person,
one of the most helpful things at a protest
you can do
you can stop
other destroying-things white people.

Elizabeth Majerus

If you are a helpful white person,
one of the most helpful protests you can do
is to publicly stop destroying,
identify you are a white person
if possible.

The white people destroying things are *not* there to help.
The white people destroying things are *not* there to help.
The white people destroying things are *not* there to help.

Robert McDonald

Irruption

When will I see you, lady of eternal and oncoming
winter, with your house cat
face
and your barred white
wings, and the curved iron blades

among the feathers
of your feet, when will you land
on the branch, or fencepost, the balcony
next to my breakfast table?
I long to see you, practitioner

of silence and hunger and smoke,
I study birding maps
online, they show where
you've perched on masts
in the harbors, on crosses

in graveyards, on crook-limbed apple trees
down by the lake—I hurried there
once, after a sighting, one
Audubon supplicant among
the many, at Montrose Point

we looked to the sky and we looked to the trees,
one woman coo-looed and clapped
her hands, as if she were searching
for her little lost dog, "Come on baby, come on"
she called out to the branches and

Robert McDonald

the slush-grey sky, she clapped her hands, as if
a snowy owl would answer, as if the owl
would descend, just like that.
What pride, when you think
you have the power

to make a ghost appear, oh raptor
of thought, oh atlas with wings
I look to the maps,
each point across the city
where you paused, and landed,

folding your own glory in
on yourself, and blinked
the amber discs
of your eyes. You
fly ahead of the killing

gusts of winter, you arrive
one hundred times all across
the city, the key on the map
is a perfect red tear.
At the forefront

of a blizzard, during this
bone-clattered, punishing year,
when will I see you, tender
sister to the snow, you
the secret lighthouse,

you the flagship to
December's armada, when
will I see you? The only
mother
left to me

in this scrapheap
of a world. You
are the ax blade,
and the hard
and singing wind.

Steve McDonald

Lesson

Even as a boy I heard the call of the bell
from the church tower that hovered above
the playground all those children who poured
into the day from their classrooms even as a boy
I heard my father hear it too the way he once
told me he wished he'd been a priest
a prayer I did not know was a prayer on his lips
in his heart the way he attended daily Mass
or prayed the rosary while driving to and from
my school aiming me even as a boy like a crossbow
at the seminary and I at thirteen saying no
I will not even as a boy I knew I did not know
and maybe did not want whatever holiness
and wisdom were I did not know what drew me
to the cracks in the flagstone like a flowering
weed until one day my knees bent before the things
of the world I turned my gaze to that weed
in bloom even as a boy I turned my gaze.

T.J. McLemore

Anthroposcenes

What color is the flesh of geology?
—Kathryn Yusoff

It floats in like a massive iceberg offshore,
a ship that rears up like a whale breaching
over a white wake. It calves smaller boats.
Pale men paddle to the village dock.
This is how the world ends,
though we don't know it yet. We cry out
and run into the surf, waving welcome,
still hoping discovery could be a mirror,
not a legend to turn earth and flesh to gold.

*

It slurps in each turn of the derrick, insectoid
as the inhuman regularity of machines
humming from every driveway, in the heart tissue
of someone we love. We forget how many times
the world's ended before us, how many worlds
we've ended to make this one ours. We suck
the juice of old apocalypses, power from flesh.
Our kids drink from the flaming tap
as we name our ending of ourselves after us.

*

It scuds overhead with the stratus clouds
as they break on the peak. Whorls of vapor
spiral down the flanks of the mountain,
passing through the trees as gentle as your hand
through a lover's tangled hair. Alpenglow
hits the shrouded peak, scattering color
to fill every fold and bough. A hush falls over
the park, the green lawn peppered with faces
looking up. Birds sing like there's no tomorrow.

Claire McQuerry

Transaction
2009

The economy came reeling
into the new year. All season

buttons plunked from old my coat—
brass coins down a dry well.

Even the clouds had turned out
their pockets. *Zilch.*

I was a ghost writer, spinning words
into dollars—a ghost, writing

from my room above the street
as traffic turned & turned like a meter

& no rain fell. *Suppose*
Pedro and Lola will buy a home,

I'd write. I'd write until my hands
went numb & my ankles swelled

& the sun rose again
over the intersection.

Another deadline in the bag. Mostly
I wrote textbooks: economics,

sales. In the dormant garden, snails
conducted their transactions with the stones.

Suppose Pedro and Lola will buy a home.
If they want optimal interest rates,

which indicators should they consider?
All across the country, the suburbs

waited — newly minted & obsolete:
the marble countertops, chandeliers,

& trash compactors. *Every conversation,*
I'd write, *is a kind of selling.*

The vacuous moon
came to rest in the trees,

where the wind tried a different
pitch on it. *When you*

persuade a friend to go
to the movies, when you ask

someone on a date, you're selling.
It's a skill you already know!

Each month, a paycheck, a new gig.
The wind blew. I couldn't stop.

Didn't I somehow have to survive?
Traffic turned & turned with the light.

Claire McQuerry

Identify the top of the sales funnel—
the words disposable & empty

as tract mansions. On the Avenue
storefronts went dark. Tents

multiplied beneath the overpasses.
When it finally rained, droplets

slammed the panes with icy
fists, demanding to come indoors.

David Melville

Tohubohu

When God clucked vowels from his belly
yowling his chutzpah and sprang
the universe open with his hullabaloo,
dawn cracked; earth was in motion,
molten, ripe, ore smelted, thudding
igneous onto ice crusts, sullen places
where ash rained on rock
meant one day to nourish meadows:
foxglove, buttercups, hollyhocks.

It was then that quick
from his throat
something dark flitted,
a blur in the eye corner.

When God jumped,
it leapt, when he crouched,
it squatted, when he ducked,
it tucked chin and dove.
When he spoke,
it was his lip mimic, yucking
the first utterance, mouthing
secret syllables, and every hollow
rang with its undercurrent.
It was a hazy wiggle,
murky, malleable.
Lucifer – God named it,
light bringer.

David Melville

And when God flung his seed,
darkness slithered
into Eve's belly, and rolled
out with the womb splat,
then crawled pudgy-armed,
a ripple across veld grass.

Each yammer, it toothed
her sore nipple; when she slept,
it dozed, then crept on tip-toe
with Adam's footpads until she woke
and the trembling
followed behind them.

When they turned, it veered,
when they laughed, it chuckled,
when they fucked, it thrust,
when they lazed, it sighed,
when they stole, it lied,
and they were happy
never quite to see it.

Henri Meschonnic
Translated from the French by Don Boes and Gabriella Bedetti

[all of life]

all of life
is a waiting room
the sky is blue I am blue
it's raining I'm raining
I drive silence
into my words
when I wait for you I wait for me
I'm encountered
by you and you
and we encounter all the others
this is how I see you
how I see myself

Robin Messing

Song of My Exile

Starving is a windless door, a fence
at my border. I need nothing more
than a sweet morsel to soldier
my suffering. My pelvis is a stone

stretched thin. The height of attainment
is weightlessness. Because womanhood
is a ravageable abundance my hips
have resisted their sensual habits.

I'm not a ship going down,
but a levitation, an absence
that cannot be harmed. I'll never
lick a spoon or be led to my death

by sensation. I trace my bones' crushed
hunger with one finger, and no one,
not even you, can make me consume
anything that proves me human.

Aksinia Mihaylova
Translated from French by Marissa Davis*

The Word

1
We take out the deepest hidden landscapes
of ourselves, pile them on the table
like two people meeting for the first
and last time—freed of future.
We smoke half a pack,
search the pile,
count the bones
taking root in our souls,
and still can't find
the word that does it.
Maybe it's the fault
of our chasms' different depths,
how they resonate with a language
unintelligible to skin.

2
Then we buy grapefruit,
stride through the Jewish neighborhood's
tight alleys, and he takes me
by the hand, he forgets me
in bookstores, he says look,
there is so much sky in the windows tonight,
pressing me against his chest
so I can't read it in his eyes:

the word,
the word that does it.

The grapefruits roll across the sidewalk.
His hands so feverous—
as if afraid of losing me,
as if afraid that I could stay.

---

* from Ciel à Perdre © Editions Gallimard, Paris, 2014

Amy Miller

Camera

Suddenly we took day trips. We were a family who toured the Old Manse, read the names of authors scratched onto windows with diamond rings. Bunker Hill and Lexington, a bridge defended in snow, black bronze statue of a farmer with a rifle. Suddenly my dad loved his camera, instamatic with a secret: If he held the button down, it made a long exposure. Now everything indoors could be remembered too, the camera steadied on the back of a pew, the rung of a Shaker chair in Sturbridge Village, where women in bonnets churned butter and a man with sideburns carved a round box on a lathe. Even the candles on my birthday cake, unlucky 13, my eyes reflecting red, three days into an ear infection but the table eternally preserved, the white plastic cups, the iced tea pitcher of green glass netted in white resin. My father now was *interested*. He had changed, my mother said; he was *enjoying things*. A trip to the Wayside Inn, its big water wheel spilling over and over. He liked these new places, she said, these old places. My sisters grown, my brothers farther, I now was an only child, silent in the back seat, feeling the dark turnpike slide by. He hadn't shouted since we moved here. The camera always rode with us, tucked in a bag. Its little eye waiting to open.

Rebecca Morton

Everything I'd Ever Seen

I hate cottage cheese. *It's good with pineapple*,
is a popular sentiment, but that's not a sustainable
position. Maybe you hate icebreakers
or scrunchies. I hate beeping, especially microwaves,
and also carpeted, ephemera-filled chain

restaurants where millions of times I've held
a man's gaze—a stuffed-in storm churning
behind his eyes—and smiled, said earnestly, *good
morning*, all because the woman I'm with—having
rearranged the mountain of condiments between us,

rehoused into the wire caddy the escaped jam
packets, gently brushed sugar-pepper-salt dust
aside—reached for my hand. *But Rebecca*, you
might say, *you don't need to smile anymore.
Things have changed.* Sure, it's better; I am less

terrified. And sometimes in the Southern
Illinois Cracker Barrel my parents frequent,
there's a kid responsible for our blueberry
pancake order who is also holding up the whole
queer world. To be honest, I'm just tired.

And I know these men. They were my teacher,
dentist, mailman. They are my family, the uncle
I only saw at Christmas who once gave each of us
a crisp, twenty dollar bill. He must have made
a special trip into town, waited in line

Rebecca Morton

at the bank. He knelt down to watch as I opened
the dopey card, found an amount of money
inconceivable to me: an amount that could buy
everything I'd ever seen a price tag on.
That's yours, he said, *Don't let your mom and dad*

tell you what to do with it. I remember exactly how
the floor lurched, and through the back patio
sliding door I saw different sorts of animals
appear above the dusk-brushed winter wheat.
They were brighter than the deer and raccoons

I knew. They were almost blinding, and with sparks.
The gray night sheltering them stretched out
past our field and the next, past the tallest
windbreak. You've probably had this experience, too,
looked up from gently shaking the last drips

of hot water through a strainer filled with noodles—
for a few, strange moments steam obscuring the view
out your kitchen window—to see your neighbor
behind her kitchen window doing the same.
Much closer than you'd ever noticed.

Simone Muench & Jackie K. White

Self-Portrait Lined by Anna Akhmatova

The secret of secrets is inside me again
spooling its prickly threads into a twine
threat, a hanging loop, or a cordon

of light around my neck as I rise, shedding
the evening from my sleeves. Asking myself,
am I the outline or the interior? Or an offering

between, like a mannequin draped each day
in another's making, with a make-shift
face, open-palm gesture, a kind of heft

against hopelessness—a supplication
to the sun gods who lead a veiled dance,
braiding shadow to silhouette, eyelet

to hook. The more the exterior resembles
the delicacy within, the quieter I can keep it,
or choose to let it rustle like a silk lining

while my silence shirrs the incandescent
curve of skin, hips wreathed in porch light.
A gold earring glitters against the dusk:

I am leaning forward into the hush, spooling
loose again, from limb and cloth and land—
I cannot tell if it is the day or the world ending.

Jason Myers

On Learning Langston Hughes Wanted His Funeral to End with "Do Nothin' Til You Hear From Me"

Whether from catgut strung across
a span of steel or wind wounded
through wood or brass we all know
a sound that knows us, that calls
& claims each moment of our lives
even in death we want a groove
to soothe that passage mellow or
mournful or wild with the liquor
of love that drips down the chin
of a song until our knees knock
like the fuzz of bees brewing roses
at times the music dims, a melody
that once took the rug from under
us now makes it no further than
our ears our hearts can break only
so many times our legs dance with
abandon one minute the next are
shamed or sicknessed to stillness
but oh when a voice or violin hits
just so a note or notes the way
sunlight turns one body of water
into a thousand coins of shimmer
we are back in Kansas or wherever
first we knew or most we felt a

presence a shivering a freedom
from the cruel belt of history
of everything not music caught
in hoarse throats & stale feet
don't you want your life your
death even to sweat with singing?

Kell Nelson

For the Union Dead

snow now boarded vegetating yellow colored girders excavations Colonel compáss-needle die soldiers frayed Soldier over When televisión Negro Colónel Aquarium

No, you don't burn. You lie perfectly still, the color of basement, your colon's steady thumping from sun up to down. You picture, on TV, a Black Christopher Columbus very close to the water.

Experimental translation of "For the Union Dead" by Robert Lowell based on the Spanish words found within the original poem.

Sarah Nichols

A*PTSD (Android Post Traumatic Stress Disorder): Bernard
After Westworld

I could be the first man
walking out of their

paradise. The last to
know I was a vessel or a
husk, a little boy falling
into rabbit holes and

then vanished. Bring
me back online. No---

take me off: my father
doesn't look like anyone
to

me, his hands full of
wires, telling me how he

made me and I would
never be other:

son
host
killer

that garden, buried,
silently reliving

Sarah Nichols

my small scenes of disaster,

easy as breathing.

Note: "Bring…back online" is used throughout *Westworld*, along with my paraphrase of "it doesn't look like anything to me," repeated by Bernard. "Host" is the term used for the robots of *Westworld* by those who run the park.

Brianna Noll

How Far Can a Memory Be Trusted?

Maybe you dreamed it or made it up.
Maybe if you lift the mask your mind
makes of things, the face behind will
say something true. Maybe in order
to be foolproof, you need to prove
a pistil is not a pistol. Various things
when piled on top of each other—
voices upon voices—come to resemble
a stretch of white reaching far beyond
the point of your eyes' discerning.
Words and sounds differ so little
from vision: they all, at their very center,
oscillate like indecisive changelings.
I think I've seen a little graying cloud
clink, as a cup set upon a saucer,
but I'm very tired. Later, it seems more like
the scrape of a spoon on the cereal bowl—
an everyday sound, a mealtime sound,
and yet when I hear it, I see not food
but rain. Isn't memory like this? A phantom
weight to remind us the brain is folded
like an accordion, creasing synapses
and thoughts into haphazard slots.
The hunter puts down his rifle, but still
he feels the cold weight of the trigger
in the crook of his finger.

Colleen O'Brien

Moving

i.

sapling's training
tube cracked & curved away
from the sapling

thought to reach out to

gaudy sun rising
behind old dead
water park

doubled then,
a Venn
in the west bus window

haystack sky mit frost don't
photograph it babe i'll only

let you down

ii.

increasingly a currency
i can't use

1 c. loose pearls provide provide

x's & v's the power
lines & vinyl siding tomb-
shaped signs on lawns WE

ARE SECURE

iii.

it's true i feel abandoned Mattress
Warehouse true i feel abandoned
Aspen Dental young

women in sunglasses captioned
start your career

Natural Stone Right Here

iv.

i like old cities where the art's been dead for decades
i like old photos full of people holding still
i like to wait pretending time must be a circle
i like to laugh at those who know that time's a line

i like it when you say you're sorry
as if to say it's true all those things happened

metal behind the trees becomes a wall of light
the sun i mean the bus moves and it's trees

Cindy Juyoung Ok

Curtain

When I say we wait on the dead I
mean star maps are sold on every corner,

because to mention color is to speak
on language. Is abstraction still luxury

in a world in which—imagine—you don't
feel watched? In the way that moral preferences are

aesthetic judgments, or how metaphor has gone out
of style. I have enough

cousins and if you've been
to an annual party for a ghost you know

most architecture is about spilling.
So people pray to be close

to the ground, spelling, as in the study
of lightning, ground and space based

measurements. Only the rich leave
bones on rice like each grain isn't

fragile. The house can also betray
by not existing (it's a tone

of boredom that leads to the kill).
Instead of romanticizing

subtlety, I dream in English with
the confidence of a private pool.

Sara Lupita Olivares

Interruptions

it is similar to a dream reaching out with certainty

calling the heron's gray shadow a shadow as it trails

through mud along the highway

in one memory, a child sleeps on the other side of the wall

in another, the ghost heaves and you continue

dropping laundry along the hallway

in the morning, we exist in propositions as if someone

were looking for the same object in a room

opening and closing, waiting and opening—to see

perhaps if it is now there

Christina Olson

Reptile House

Doesn't matter which zoo or city:
        the reptile house always takes first
in the Least Popular Exhibition
        of the Zoo contest. I go to it first—
just me and the other sweaty people,
        the exhausted elderly, the breastfeeding.
And me, childless and tall. Frogs
        are not reptiles but you'll find them
in the reptile house. In seventh grade
        I fell in love with *Dendrobatidae*,
poison dart frog. Tiny deadly jewels
        in their velvet green boxes. That side
of the reptile house was always wet,
        fronds dripping. Even then I called
the spikes of ferns *fronds*. I had to
        be known as smart, because smart
was all I had. That and crooked teeth,
        thick glasses. I had new braces
that turned my smile into a silver EKG,
        a favorite store that the other girls
in my new class, through snickers, let me know
        was a *thrift* store. In the reptile house,
other people can only see the outline
        of your hometrimmed bangs, can't read
any of the labels on your clothes.
        Snake eyes don't have eyelids—
they have a scale called, of course,
        a *spectacle*. Snakes don't blink,
give nothing away. I was in middle school—
        of course I recognized that

disinterest when it held me in its gaze.
           You can spend a half day in the reptile house
and only see three things move.
           You learn to be patient, to breathe
like you're meditating. I never
           touched the glass in the reptile house—
instead, I ran my sore tongue over
           and over the metal in my mouth.
The orthodontist promised that braces
           would soon charm my teeth into order.
In the reptile house, I longed for fang.

Pablo Otavalo

Vigil
for Carlos

The hum of the oxygen pump
filling your lungs drowns
the whimpers of my sisters
around your bed. Your hand,
unmoving, on the stark linen
like the broad hands
of Michelangelo's Moses. I

       can't look into the night sky
       for my grandmother's god;

after the last impulse cascades
your nerves I'll lose you
to carbon and decay. We spoke
of it once, under a summer sun,

       a cigar in your heavy hand burning
       right through you. *Lo unico que hay*

es hoy y ayer. Today and yesterday
is all we get. You carried old songs,

old drums, old chains, from an island
you never got to see again. I can't

       look into the night sky towards
       that ancient light without
       feeling myself getting smaller
       and smaller, nearly falling

off the turning earth. I craft
a prayer like a balsa raft

          on a formless sea, for I can't
          keep you out there, adrift—

Rachelle Parker

Echoes of Coarse Fabric

Sitting in my work cubicle, I hear a shriek, a slam
and cussing. I know that the copy machine
has gotten jammed again and wonder
how many sheets of the paper have been pulled
out and splotched with toner. I look back
to my Excel spreadsheet. The numbers start to blur
and I see my reflection in the monitor. My Brooks
Brothers suit, the one I got during the after Christmas
sale, begins to dissolve leaving me bare

save for a narrow cotton strap of a shift. My hands
begin to fill with its tattered hem. Then I am barefoot,
running across the soil-colored carpet squares.
The corridor flanked with file cabinets, bound
to concrete walls with large nuts and bolts,
have become tobacco rows. The green leaves
lined with loopers tickling my ears.

I hear there's gone be a delivery and head
to the receiving area. A courier already there
holds a box and bellows he's got a shipment
fresh off a steamer all the way from H. & D.H. Brooks
& Co., Cherry Street, New York. He reads off the bill
of lading: 100 stout and heavy woolen
dresses, winter gray. He say "the master
of the house will need to sign."

Standing in the clearing, my feet now
dusty, I's hope dere's shoes fo' me.

Genevieve Payne

At Georgia's House Party

When a thing has just ended:
a song, the night, my friend's brief
life, that's when I feel it most.

From across the hall, bug lights
touch the cheeks
of a few people I know.

In quiet rooms we grow
quiet too and close
like flowers close.

On the porch I watch
a man break bottles in the drive.
The sound warms the dark
as pieces flare onto the grass and tar,
holding street light. Not the event
but the act of remembering.

Even time breaks up. Not pain
but the memory of pain. Not the bottle
but the memory of it, whole and still and safe,
like an eye shut in the dark.

Cecilia Pinto

[Joyous]

Joyous
the pigeons at Pulaski and Lawrence, too many to count too many to count too
           many too many to count
     swoo
         ping across the intersection back and forth between the dingy corner buildings
  the   the   the
building   building   building
with a bar   with a phone store   with a dollar store   and the corner with a bus
                                                                                     stop and look,
the
   cars
      trundle
          across
       the streets
          im   patient ly.

But the birds fly backandforth in great silver-gray groups   across the
intersection toomanytocount
resting briefly
               on building tops or arched street lights like in a
                                  e
                            h d
                         t   r
                      a   a
                    c   l.

     Then they fly again. Maybe they startle.
     Maybe it's for fun. Just fun!

The four of us stand at a corner, Renee and Jeff and Jim and me.

The birds fly above us but   we can feel the energy they are using.
                    closenough

Our hearts beat faster   too fast to count, to count, to count.

They see us. The pigeons see us with their eyes.
We are startled. We have eyes too and hearts. They have hearts.
Here we are at the intersection of Pulaski and Lawrence
the pigeons are here and   here   here and
this here is word and
                                            t e s t i m o n y o f r e v e l a t i o n .

Cecilia Pinto

Nurse

The corpse of your horse needs to go home.
        I don't know what to do with my hands.
Wreathe the body in military ribbons, wrap up the red roan

in black, the black in gold, the battle blue in darker tones.
        I cannot say that these were ever my plans.
The corpse of your horse needs to go home

to rest in pastures green and grown.
        Someone else might have taken a stand.
Instead, wreathe the ribboned body, I will wrap the red roan.

Again the endless violence; the arrow, the bullet, the drone.
        The pretty ribbons flutter in the wind.
The corpse of your horse needs to go home.

These are the bodies bloated, ballooned, alone.
        How do we mourn the wet red weight of all our dead?
Wreathe the bodies in ribbons as we wrap up the roan.

Lift and carry, grip and groan.
        This is all we can do with our hands.
The corpse of your horse needs to go home.
Wreathe the body in ribbons, wrap up, wrap up the red roan.

Megan Pinto

Seascape with Father

We ride the train through Mumbai
        and I fall asleep. At Churchgate, my Father
                and I sit and watch the sea.

I am seventeen and waiting to become.
        The whole plane ride over, I flip
                through glossy college catalogues,

stare at the green expanse of campus
        lawns and red gold maple leaves: a perfect
                East Coast fall. I am trying to imagine

my new life when I am returned
        to the place of my parents' birth. I tell
                my Father that the beach in Mumbai

reminds me of Miami, where we drink
        from coconuts through straws. In Miami,
                my Father shows me how to cleave meat

from the coconut and we lick juice
        from our palms. By the time I leave
                for college, my Father will not speak to me.

Years later, when I call my Father
        from New York, I will walk to the East River
                and show him my view of the city. Through our phones

we will look at each other, and the estuary,
        and maybe I will tell him how once, in college,
                I tried to write down everything I knew of his life

and only filled a page.

Susan Azar Porterfield

J.M.W. Turner, *Slavers Throwing overboard the Dead and Dying— Typhoon coming on*

The leg is delicate enough to be female, chained
by an iron anklet

           *

cut free   under the roiling, still alive
yet alive we guess

           *

      that small, seen foot thrills sharp
as a dancer's, tense with blood   terror's
what's wanted

           *

      purple/blue storm-light, storm clouds
against whose chest we beat,

           *

carried off, cut loose, tossed out—

           *

the guilty ship struggles to write
its story too   already a ghost.

Meg Reynolds

We Are Happy

The other morning	your father and I were in our underwear
making carrot cake.	Your dad washed the white mixing bowl,
then sprayed me	with water while I searched for the tablespoon.
I laughed, called him	shithead, and he pressed me to him there
in the tiled kitchen,	a thin film of water warming between us
after we made love	for the first time since the miscarriage.
I made a choice	to witness this, kiss your father,
to forgive him	for his body and what happened in my body alone,
for everything	it was impossible for him to know. I accept
the secret of this	as he holds me around it and heats up the kettle.
I want you to know	that we are happy
even as I	resist fetching you from the toilet bowl
to press you	between the pages of a book, save you
the way my mother	saved my baby teeth in a paper box. Even as I search
and search the water,	bent down in the bathroom, looking for us on you.
Our doctor called them clots, but they are parts, more than knots	
of blood settling	at the bottom. You are bright vermillion like a poppy.
That's what we	used to call you when you were alive
and your father	put his big hand on my belly to say goodbye before work.
You were the size	of a poppy seed and your heart cells practiced beating.
They blinked	in the second ultrasound like you were waving.

Rainer Maria Rilke
Translated from the German by Donald Mace Williams

Buddha

As if he heard. Silence: a thing far away . . .
We can no longer hear it as we pause.
And he is Star. And over him array
themselves huge stars, invisible to us.
Oh he is All. Truly now, should we wait
for him to see us? Would he feel the need?
And if before him we should fall prostrate,
he, like some creature, would stay numb and deep.
For that that wrenches us all to his feet
for countless years has circled through him thus.
He, who forgets what pain we feel
and undergoes what exiles us.

Liana Sakelliou
Translated from the Greek by Don Schofield

The Italian Circus on the Moraitiki Shore

Loud music,
all of us applauding—
oh, what a wonder to see Mike Lamar
in top hat, tux and white gloves,
twirling a cane in his hands,
then letting it hover
on its own
in circles around his body.
When the elephant sauntered off
toward the sea, unperturbed,
looking for water, it sank
deep into the sand.
We all gathered around
its huge head
stuck in mud, struggling fiercely.
The performance suspended,
we posed for pictures with the monkeys,
till the circus hands brought ropes
and tied them around the elephant's huge body.
Wailing in desperation,
it kept turning its trunk
round and round in the air,
like Mike Lamar's cane.

Liana Sakelliou
Translated from the Greek by Don Schofield

Marine Education at the Beginning of the Twentieth Century

In this wooden hut
I am putting on
a one-piece bathing suit
and a cap. Mornings,
I swim for hours.
The algae kiss the starfish
and curl up,
while the urchins
without moving
kiss me,
exciting me all over
with the words they whisper
to my flesh.
Nearby—
small willows, eucalyptuses
and a dock for my lover
to berth his boat.

Stewart Shaw

Plants and Trees
*for Eric Garner**

Hardened trunks/beating/bearing witness/winsome willows/weeping/withering in winter/yew/plums itself/yellow and yawning sweetly awake/yet blossoms with/a yearning for air/black roots/breaching distance/reaching/speaking to other entangled roots/embrace the oaks they could not save/breach the streets and sidewalks/cement breathes/with the trees/lungs sweetened by oxygen/breathe with/him/for him/

The plants convene/a shebeen/a juke joint gathering/sing green spaces/open/drink and share/stories/tobacco/still holding death/tight/the darkness/of oxygen deprived lungs/is again disinvited/stands blue and black/in dusky light/while the other plants/breathe in and/out/empty their bellows/their bellicose lungs/into the world/breathe so the rest can/refuse the notion/of deprivation/the belief/that anything should go without air///

---

* Eric Garner
On July 17, 2014, Eric Garner died in the borough of Staten Island after police officer Daniel Pantaleo put him in a prohibited chokehold while arresting him. Garner was being arrested on the suspicion of selling loose cigarettes from packs without tax stamps.

Carrie Shipers

Performance Review: "You seem to really struggle with the culture here"
After Dan Lyons

We've never seen you use a standing desk
or play in our sandbox. You insist
the nap rooms are ridiculous, which suggests
you aren't giving enough to really feel
depleted. When we asked you to wear
your corporate hoodie once a week,
we meant in addition to Friday. We agree
you don't look good in Big Bird yellow,
but it's vital our brand stands out.
You decline too many meetings you're
invited to. You claim you can't contribute
to projects you know nothing about,
but cross-collaboration is a core value.
Technically there are no wrong results
to the personality exams, but we'd prefer
you weren't a triple introvert, an XFU
and the color brown. You spit out
awesomesauce, *snowflake* and *rock star*
as though they taste bitter, interrupt
our praise for drinking the Kool-Aid
by mentioning mass murder.
You weren't required to sky-dive
because of your cast, but you should've
been at the Lego art tequila party.
Even in our custom font, there's something
off about your exclamation points.

The more of them you add, the sadder
we become. That's probably why
you don't get cheers from peers,
picked to share a desert island with.
You're usually called chum, and not
in a nice way. You may have memorized
the Founders' pets, birthdays and sacred
principles, but you need to sing them
on-key and fervently. Instead,
you laugh at your contract's *delightion*
clause and won't agree that 1 and 1
make 3. Saying someone's fired feels
really uncool, so we're hoping you'll resign.

Sarah Dickenson Snyder

Entering The Odyssey

I like thinking of Penelope,
watching her weave and unweave,
maybe see Athena slip into her
room, hover over the bed built
into a tree, ease her into dream.
See the stone ledge of her window
lined with a white-tipped feather,
milky curves of shells, and small bones
like something on our kitchen sill—
a wishbone among the dust
and keys and curled rubber bands.
The furcula, what a bird needs to pull its wings
up and down. My mother dried it
in the sun, the arched "v" reminding me
of the skeletal remains of a tiny angel's
cast-off wings, where it awaited
the breaking and wish-granting.
The weight of waiting, of anticipating
who gets the larger part, my small
index finger being brave,
willing to have a wish unmet.
So much in what vanishes, too much to count—
who has more cherry pits in the bottom of her bowl,
who gets the paper ring of a grandfather's cigar,
who holds her breath the longest in that under-
world of water—will we ever get what we want?
Maybe all hopes arrive in disguise
like an old beggar.

Jennifer Sperry Steinorth

Her Read

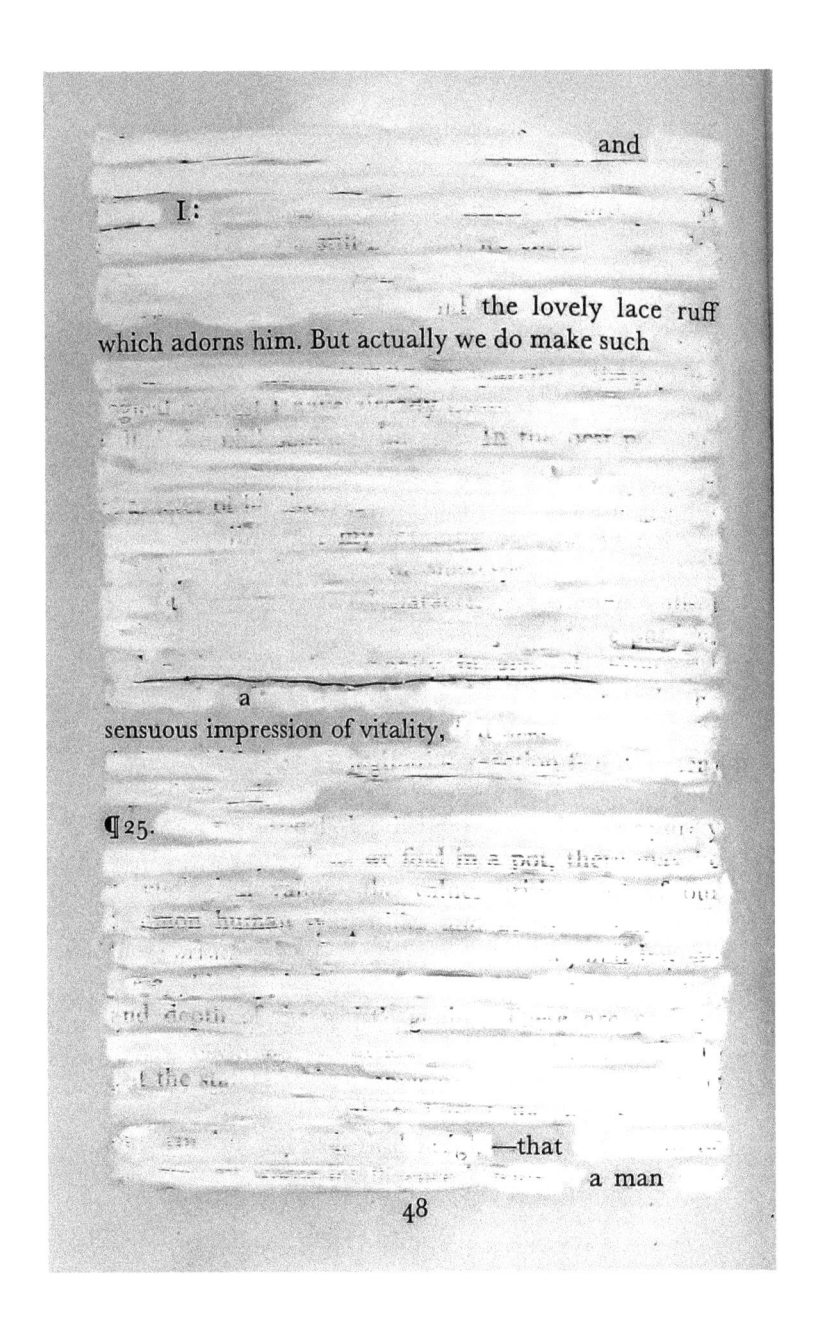

and

I:

the lovely lace ruff
which adorns him. But actually we do make such

a
sensuous impression of vitality,

¶ 25.

—that
a man

Jennifer Sperry Steinorth

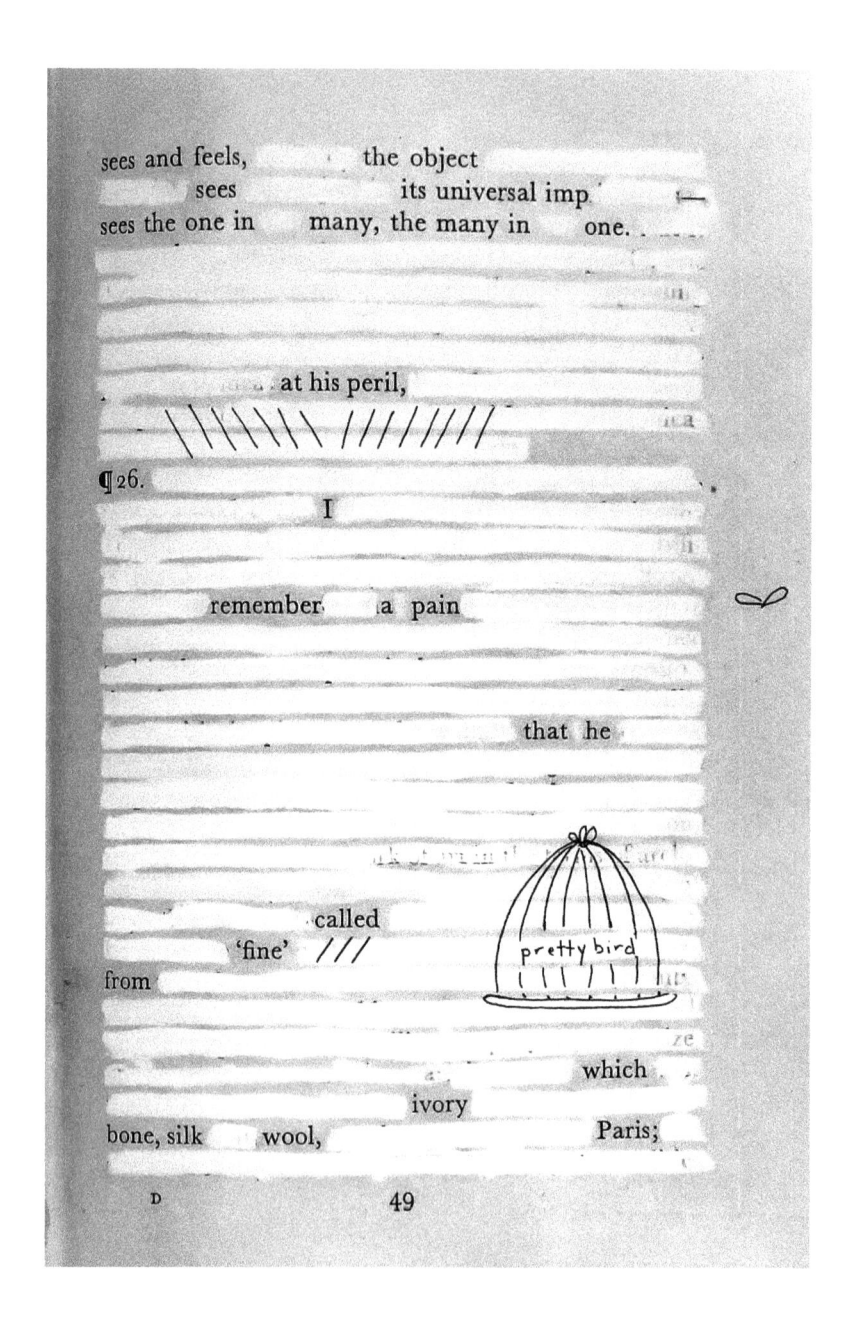

sees and feels,   the object
     sees   its universal imp.
sees the one in   many, the many in   one.

at his peril,

\\\\\\\\ ////////

¶ 26.
           I

remember   a pain

that he

called
'fine' ///   *pretty bird*
from

                        which
          ivory
bone, silk   wool,   Paris;

The ass is

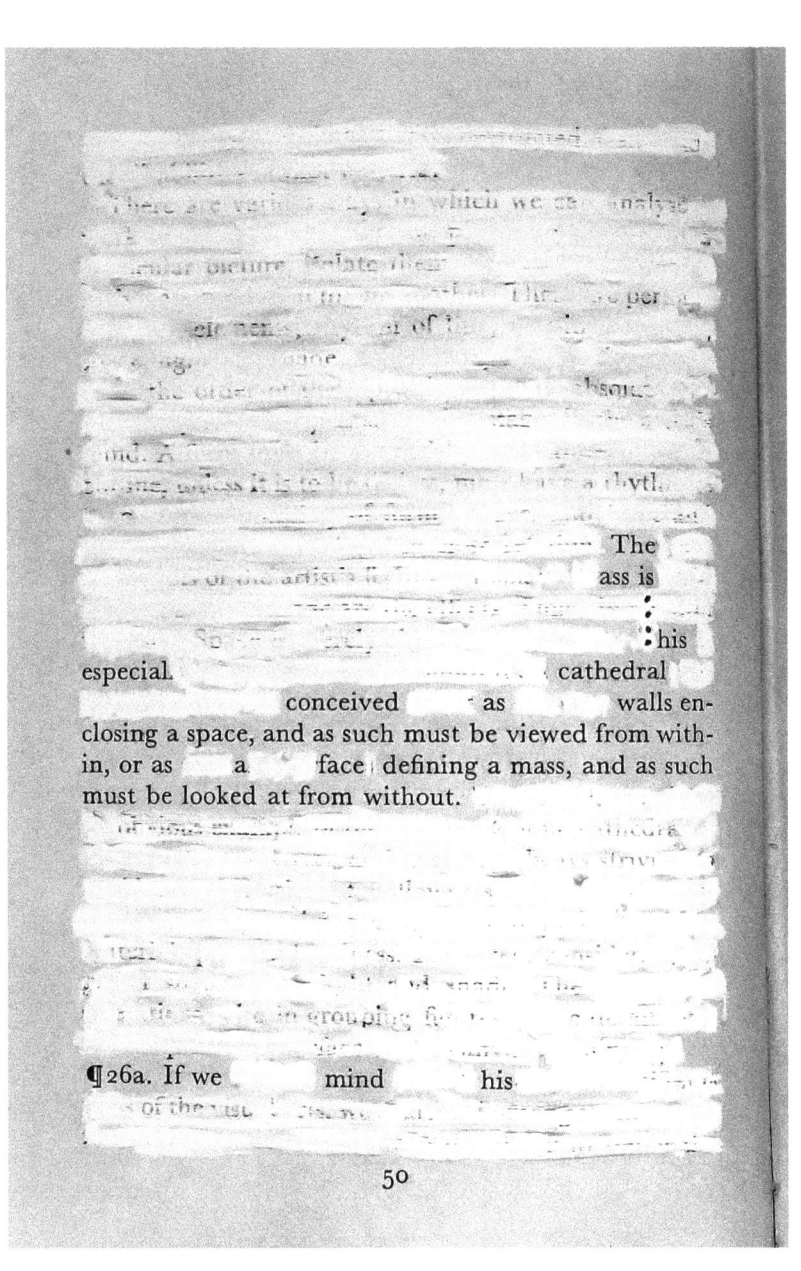

his

especial cathedral

conceived as walls enclosing a space, and as such must be viewed from within, or as a face defining a mass, and as such must be looked at from without.

¶ 26a. If we mind his

Jennifer Sperry Steinorth

        rose and

passage
his
                                      child

amusingly he relates how

Pain

is

in the hands of a master

How
can

we who imagine ourselves dancing

express
the continuous
edge

break off at just the right point   re-enter the body

without offending the
conventional codes   for example, the   manners   of trees
and   the

Jennifer Sperry Steinorth

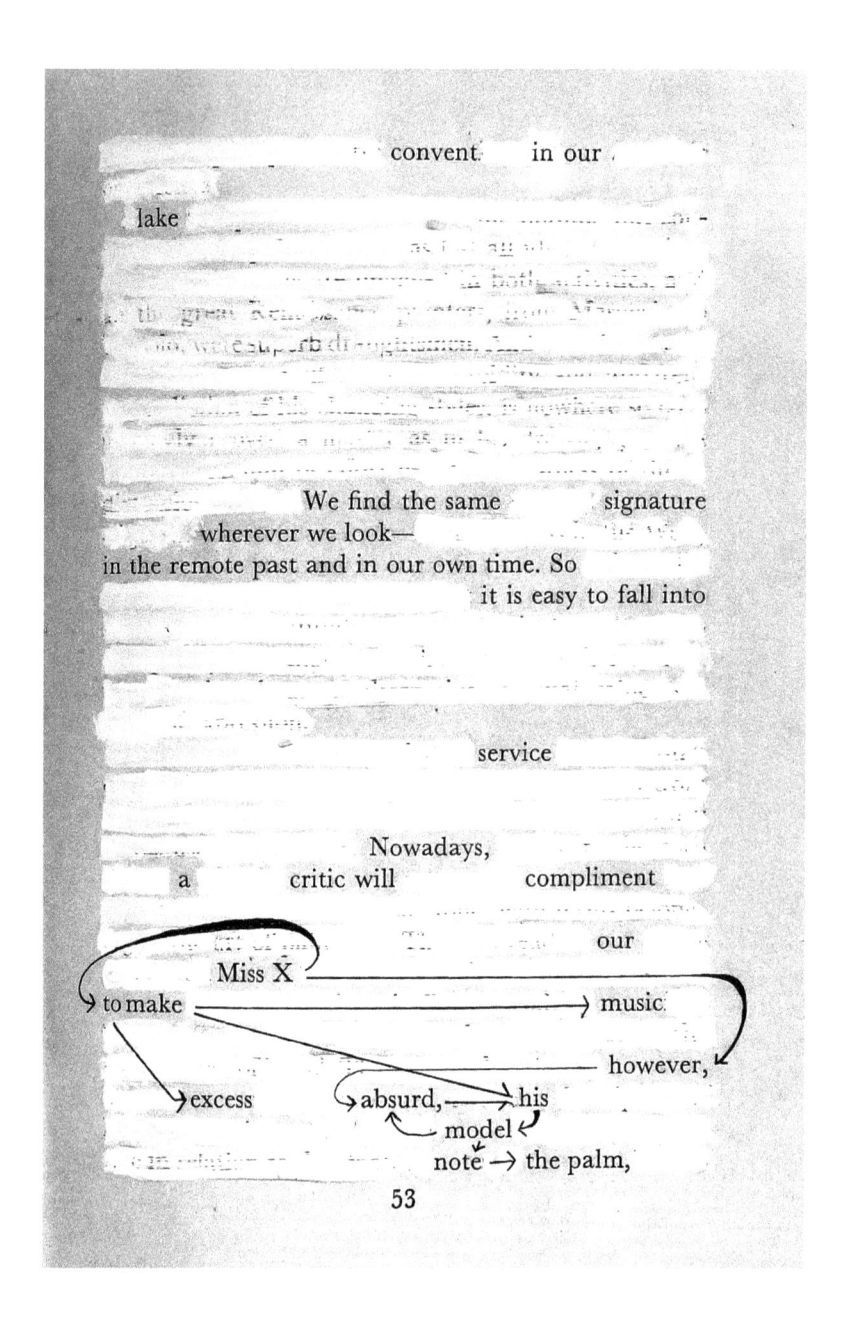

                    convent   in our

lake

        We find the same   signature
        wherever we look—
in the remote past and in our own time. So
                        it is easy to fall into

                service

        Nowadays,
  a   critic will   compliment
                      our
      Miss X
→ to make   → music
                      however,
→ excess   → absurd, → his
             model
            note → the palm,

53

R skin made
me one in pain : I understand two
things by the word *one*: first, the exact relief
of objects against each other in
darkness, as they are near or . . .

. . . secondly, the exact
colour of

A

white and black

pig

Jennifer Sperry Steinorth

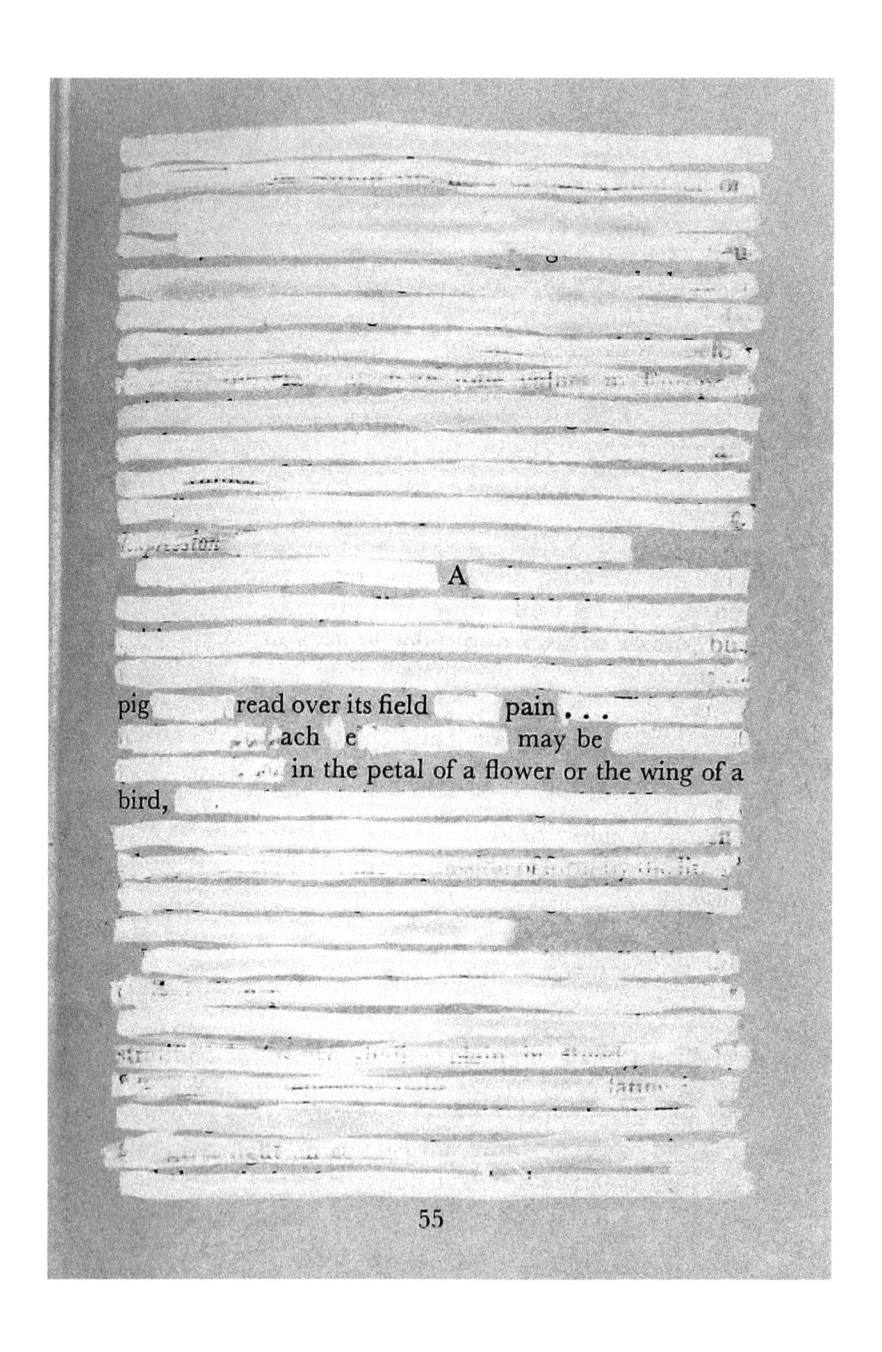

A

pig   read over its field   pain . . .
    ach e   may be
        in the petal of a flower or the wing of a
bird,

Even Leonardo,
had to

touch
my
whole,

'open window', as it has been called,

with

his
manual dexterity
and a scientific aim at feeling
me
n o t

in control of his

effects.

Jennifer Sperry Steinorth

"Her Read" is an erasure/reconstruction of Herbert Read's "The Meaning of Art" first published in 1931.

Noah Stetzer

A Two-Body Problem

It was a television I think that said Voyager
had left the heliosphere: crossing into what they called
the heliopause: a silent empty where solar wind
no longer makes a difference; that river delta
where freshwater sunlight dissolves into the saltwater
gulf of interstellar space—there the sun's hot exhale
at last gives out. Who even thinks about Voyager:
a sling-shot pilgrim on its way for how long now,
that obedient clockwork with regular far away sights
and sounds—good old Voyager—but here it's come
—or gone—farther even to an icy brink, into its own faint
shadow out front against the dark. Has it been hours
or days since you've been here? My nurse
says that patients in the ICU aren't usually conscious
—she doesn't know why they even have TVs. This kind
of room's never all the way quiet: something important
clicks or beeps, a light comes on goes off, numbers
flash on the black monitor—my heart and my lungs
work and work. This kind of an *always* room
you never think of: like the way someone's *always*
got an eye on Titanic rusting at the bottom of the ocean
or those guards *always* at the Tomb of the Unknowns
counting twenty-one steps this way then back—
whether you think about it or not, *always* someone
between awake and asleep in a bed
in the ICU. I'm too adrift to count back or up,
has it been days or hours since you'd been here;
were you back at our little house with dishes
in the sink, dirty clothes on the floor, our empty house
with just you keeping one foot in front of the other
turning from floor to floor, to room to desk to chair

Noah Stetzer

circling round for what you can't remember. My nurse
with her gloves and mask— the HIV so far gone
my immunity's as thin as the fabric across her mouth
—she comes and goes to blow on the embers
of my last few t-cells and now she's here to push
morphine into my line—*for pain* she says *for sleep*
— we've both had enough of me asking *how long
has it been* and *how far have I gone*; has it been a day
or just an hour; no window and the lights don't let
you know; poor Voyager out at nothing's doorstep
sending back its useless static. *Count back* she says
start from ten—and the pneumonia makes it hard
to breathe—*deep breaths* she says *say nine* she says—
but I'm no pilgrim on an arrow straight line
—*say eight* she says *say seven*—I'm not built
to go very far and you and me are what they call
a two-body problem—*say six* she says—circles
circling one with just the other—*say five*—faces
always facing the same side—*say four* she says—
maybe like magnets or gravity or some thing with numbers
—*say three*—so what looks like leaving
what might be escape—*say two* she says—something
stops and swings me round—*say two say two*—
a call a thought some bit of string to bring
me home.

Keli Stewart

How to Read Tea Leaves

I keep toilet-gazing into the tea leaves of a fetus divining bitter root, blood flooding feet.
All your pulpy tendrils spun into a dime, tiny and not-yet named girl-child, shape-shifting
in a small toilet cypher. I'm three months into this love affair and throw myself downstairs twice.
Once, mimicking a girlhood, in a spinning house, the second, I ate pennyroyal and clover, trying to
disappear you into stardust and clay, hoping that you'd come back, in time.
Will you ever come back to me, now that I am my own bad mother and you, a letting, your
black eyes swirl in stool. I'm deciphering catastrophe. My slow breath marked by yours.

Keli Stewart

on turning 30

during my midday inadequacy,
i sit in my chair and look
at my hands & wonder if my hands
will beat my children & if my
children will flee from my house
& i wonder while my hands
are drowned in dishwater if i might
one day want a little bit of cocaine to calm me
& if i will ever need a bit of cocaine to calm me
between oprah & the price is right
& if my house will ever be clean &
if i will go to the basement to
clean up a lot & i wonder if i will
cuss

and lock my husband out for days
& beat my children & then forget
so that my mouth will forget sorry.
if I will hug them afterwards
so that my son becomes more
frightened of my touch than what
is in his closet & grows up to love
white women
& if they will call only on mother's day
& new year's because someone
told them to & if they will shroud
their mirrors in black cloth
before i am dead.

Stephanie Lane Sutton

Palindromes

Sexes is chiral, like chemistry or insect wings.
It begs the question: do geese see god? A dog
sees geese in grayscale and cannot spell
its own name backward. Madam, in Eden
we're even. Red delicious. My mouth, a moth.
Your mouth, lit til noon. Moon on the sheets.
Spill. Lull. Lips. So much symmetry in hands.
When they touch: a reflection one may hold.
When you're gone I feel like a lonely tylenol.
My thigh, your thigh, my thigh, your thigh.
No melon, no lemon. No gods, no heaven.
It begs the question: won't lovers revolt now?
I'm a poem—open me. You, opening—a poem.
Like a mirror, I won't look away til you do.

Jason Tandon

Writing

Those three nut heads
on the furnace filter panel
are loose and stripped.
Mornings I come down
to the back storage room
where I have a desk
and a green banker's lamp,
boxes of Mirado pencils
and yellow legal pads.
By now, when the furnace fires up,
I've grown used to those
three nut heads
and their high-pitched glee.

Maya Tevet Dayan
Translated from the Hebrew by Jane Medved

Cotton

When I imagine my childhood as perfect,
I remember you
and me, on a stack of cotton in the kibbutz,
small and raised up like two cherries
on top a mountain of whipped cream.

I conceal the swarm of bees
and my fear of them, the persistent
humming that saws towards us,
the sweat dripping down our backs,
the weight of the heat on our eyelids,
the itch that climbs from our feet to our necks,
the asbestos walls of the cotton barn
closing in on us like a chimney.

I blur the fear of heights,
the worry that we will suddenly stop breathing
from all the cotton fibers pressing the air,
and because you don't always need a reason
to stop breathing.

I erase everything I didn't know
then, everything that happened to you
on quiet nights without bees,
outside of this whiteness,
when you weren't on a soft peak,
and not in daylight,
and not with me, and not alone,
the windows of your body broken
wide open with night.
All those terrible nights.

Maya Tevet Dayan

There remains only our legs burrowing
into the whitest fluff,
our skinny knees, bones stretching
under the skin, far

from any portion of darkness.
We float above an abyss of silence,
bits of cotton in our hair. You smile –
your two front teeth leaning on each other,
like the slats of a broken fence.

Lee Colin Thomas

Stride

      if it's me
                i'll always walk

like the giraffes
    on television   unencumbered

by anything more than
      a necklace of birds

and my always sunshot conversation
    with whatever's divine

in the sky over the savannah: why
    make me

this way, oh great one?   why
    this unruly clatter

of limbs marrowed with sugar
    and worry?

why doom me   forever
    a spectacle

of the watering hole?   why not
    raise the trees from their roots

and teach them to amble about
    if you need to be so

Lee Colin Thomas

entertained.   why why   enough
      to choke the seventh foot

of my throat.   i know what you'll
      say, lord goddess soul-

spinner salt-prince   air-mother.
      and i admit   i'm happy

more days than not.   i'm grateful the sweet
         leaves yield

and lie down   on my tongue.
      no one moves a body like this one

on a whim.   maybe just once
      you could acknowledge that

getting up to another quiet morning
      like this no matter how

beautiful
         is still some

incredible feat. i see for miles
      in every direction   and i'll

keep walking.   every movement
      so composed   even you'll

believe i know exactly
      where it is i'm going.

Cedric Tillman

Feed My People (The Toxicology Prayer)

Father we come to you again because another dead black man is on the news. Lord I ask that by this time tomorrow we'll find out he didn't need money, that he had a regular job and not a side hustle, that you'll close up the mouths of the reporters fixed on telling us he was broke. Make him worthy of mercy Lord, not one of these people selling burnt CDs or loose cigarettes outside the store, or passing potentially fake bills—Lord I pray he sold no death penalty weed, that he has no kids who could use the money. We ask that he doesn't have asthma or COVID so the cause of death can be the officer's knee, or the officer's forearm, or the officer's gun. Lord we ask there be no PCP or TCP or THC in his blood, Lord we bind TCB 'cause we know anyone who'd put that in their head tends to end up being a threat. May no mention of Chicago without a mention of the Great Migration and redlining and contract housing formed against him prosper. Lord I pray he wasn't too dark since it was nighttime, I pray he light as Steph Curry. I pray he followed the president on Twitter and played some kind of ball in college or high school—make it so Father, you know what they like. I pray the truth saves them money, that their lies are expensive. Lord I pray Breonna didn't have a drink before bed lest they say it made her too sluggish to dodge bullets. They'll say but for the alcohol she'd have answered the door, that any substance that can muffle telepathy could lead to muted magic. Lord I pray that if she was on Lisinopril or statins or birth control that she missed a couple days, make her clean in their sight. In his mug shot, may her boyfriend pass for someone the NRA deems worthy of the right to defend a home, may his piss test come back positive for living waters. Oh Lord, wash us white enough to be mourned. Suffer us the coping mechanisms. For you know how they absolve themselves. If there are traces of escape in our blood, they will say we got what we deserved.

Rodrigo Toscano

The Revolution

Gray birds made of marble falling from the sky

Swamp oaks taking two steps forward, if you look closely

Levee water levels rising exactly by four feet

New bridges made of glass suddenly appear over urban canals

Storefront signages swapping places, making sense

Picnics two feet below sea level — in the thousands

Girls with brown eyes rolling boulders into pyramids of gold

Girls with blue eyes casting steel hooks onto silver gates

Girls with green eyes forming a field of grass to skip on

Red, chrome-out chopper cruising the streets, no rider

Purple sun painting twelve windows onto local birthing center

Hell, the word, the concept, scaring no children at this hour

Heaven, the word, the concept, wood cube in dank attic, rotting

Two-minute clip of brawny man battling an alligator in loop mode

One-minute clip of young boy twirling brawny man in loop mode

Sundown western breeze fanning ice tower evaporations

Blank stare of a statue on an iron barge seaward bound

Bats across a full moon portrait in a trash bin flaming

Canoe made of pure sugar gliding over asphalt streets at midnight

Thirty second clip of diamond-toothed baby in loop mode

Bayou bugs onto a fourth generation since yesterday morning

Yellow birds made of polyurethane come to a consensus

Fifteen second clip of upside-down city skyline

Justice, the word, vision, in an orange cloud, distending, glowing

Seven and a half second clip of pencil frolicking on white paper

Four-hundred-foot mound of multicolored masks and panties toppling

Deceased couple with brass canes crossing glass bridge at dawn

Traffic barricades napping again, if you take a glance

Jess Turner

In The Acred Woods

I want to tell you something honest. The child died

       in the snow.   The father blew bubbles

in the kitchen.

Red mittens found in the acred woods.   I am

                  looking

for a sign.

        Mother listened to the father speak

    through a vent

in the floor: *She's a good mother, but*

            a terrible wife.

The child caught fire in the snow.

The signal tower blinked through the cold night,

        mother pressed to the vent

    like a crow

to wind.   I want to tell you something honest:

mother died

with the child in the snow— two crows

leaning

into air.

He was in the kitchen and then he was not.

Stephen Tuttle

Elijah Fed by Ravens

When you think of Elijah and his beard of twigs you think of the ravens that brought him bread and meat twice daily. Who could eat such scavenged food, delivered uncleanly? You think of the woman he met at the edge of a river run dry, both of them thirsty as salt cedar. She baked for him from depleted stores, making of nothing sufficiency. But then, of course, her son fell breathless into death. You think of that son and you think of your brother, whose lungs in x-ray were full of light. You think of Elijah on the unsteady mountain, among fierce wind and fiercer flame. You think of the emptiness that came his way. What some have called a whisper and others a silence. You think of your brother at the very end, his body a weakening bellows. The rattle, when it came, was closer to a snore. You remember him as a child in your grandfather's garden, beyond the last row of snap peas he ever planted. Your brother spies a cluster of robins on a fence post. In his hands an air rifle. You think you know how this story ends, but you wonder if you've got it right. After all, every time you call it to mind, Elijah is there, drifting heavenward in his chariot of fire, higher and still higher until you lose him in the sun. Your brother takes aim, hoping not to kill but to force flight.

Enrique S. Villasis
Translated from the Filipino by Bernard Capinpin

Muro Ami

The scent of newly mown grass in the morning has become foreign to my nose. After all, my breath has taken in gasoline and fumes for many months; vapor as salt, earth as rust, and if our step should have something to anchor on, it was more often on a slippery particle board or scaly cement, while we couldn't call that which grazed the light a moth if the sea didn't lend itself to its name; in those times, contrary to experience, even Captain's tied roosters have become hoarse in the confusion run by time. Perhaps, this was the purpose of loneliness. Better for those who've returned earlier to the sand. What was certain was that our hairs have forgotten how to stand on end, and if one closes one's eyes, while mending the greying nets, what could be heard was a mountain's snoring coming from an invisible and unreachable island, or sometimes, the sigh from a kiss from one cloud to another, the last ripple from a plunging comet, the wail of broken coral oftentimes blamed for having stung the eye: small comebacks, restrained grievances. Always, a heavy chest during moments of rest, the cold cloaking us, the salt on the skin glittering, ache scrawling on the lashes, and after, the resurgence of danger that twists our gut under the sea, bridging its navel to ours. It is between moments of waiting that we find ourselves—the shadows of coconut leaves comb over the hairline while the currents are waving from afar, an alluring braid of our small tragedies.

Sara Moore Wagner

How to Survive It

You'll have to do it again, dig out the bright
bulbs you planted as a child, daffodils
still blooming like bubbles,
light mornings where there's nothing
to do but plant and replant every seedling,
the sprouting eye of tomato wedged
against the window, the robin's egg.
You'll have to put yourself back
into bed, teach your legs to thin
and shorten, will your hair to soft
out and lighten like corn silk, then back
in the husk of your mother, back when
someone knew how to care for you
by just carrying you. Figure out
where you came from, then tell me
where I came from, wherever you end
up, floating in a basket over the bed
where your parents dreaded morning,
how it came on and they got up.
I know we can't do anything
but get up, can't even retrace the steps
you took to meet me that night
when you said everything has been
building to this moment where we're locked
inside with our children in a single long day.
You say, *what did we do to deserve
this*. What is this. If we can't go back,
what is there but an evening
where I put eggs in a cart online
and pray they show up in the morning.

John Sibley Williams

Self-Portrait as Lacuna

What do we do with a body
                severed from other bodies,

with a child who cannot weave herself
                into & out of embrace?

When the plastic stars glued to her ceiling
                supplant the celestial, dreams

& hungers cast only so high, prayers smacked
                hard against drywall & blue paint?

Into the burn barrel out back, everything I hoped
                would someday wear her name. Family,

only a state away, already dimming to memory. Only
                my face to remind her of her own.

A miniature dollhouse world, prematurely on fire. This
                afflicted air. Breath. When breathing

becomes the barbed fence between neighbors.
                Cover yourself, love. Please.

It is my splintered cross to keep you safely distanced
                from humanity. Here, another promise

I didn't mean to break. Here, another kiss as apology.
                A board book to show what it was like

John Sibley Williams

before. Talking animals to prove the world can be
                wildly unquiet. & innocent. A sky

made up of myths. & stars. Honest-to-goodness stars.
                All gas & flame & unobstructed whimsy.

Here is someone else's tree to carve your initials into.
                Here, love, is the tree of my body

to learn to climb. Far from here. From me. To touch
                whatever's still up there, beautifully above us.

Daniel Woody

euphemisms

you're still in the fold *he*
says assuring me of my blackness
on a corner in chicago *he*
points out the beauty of my floral shirt *i*
thank him say unfortunately sears
has gone out of business sears
has broken my heart *you*
must be an artist *you*
are still in the fold *i*
don't care what anyone else says
you're still in the fold *he*
adds clarifies revises
there are all kinds of brothas *he*
looks through me before looking away
an artist to him is a euphemism
for queerness *i*
pass through anger instantly
perceive the encounter as an expression
of confidence solidarity connection
of coming out good luck *i*
say which is my own euphemism for stay
sane in a world in which souls are stolen stay
safe in a world in which we are hunted stay
in other words soft

William Winfield Wright

Evaporation

Your grandfather forgets
he was a horse thief.

Your father forgets
he was a drunk.

Your sister stops explaining
why she resented your parents

for playing favorites.
The cousins you wished death on?

Well, they're dead now
and so are you.

The church fathers wasted all that time
telling us that purgatory hurts,

making an airtight case for the need
to be shrieved or harrowed,

wrung out of our impurities
before getting in here,

like showering ahead of the pool
or putting on clean underwear

in case you end up in the hospital.
With all the time in the universe,

there's no point barbequing anyone.
The sun will do that regardless

of prophecy or the collective unconscious.
It's bright and there's no atmosphere.

Whatever we try to hold on to
is going to disappear anyway.

For those who try to hang on
to metaphors,

we're just the dark speck that gets
into the snow globe,

the small fly resting on the business end
of the log they use to ring the temple bell.

Each of us will shrink and evaporate,
growing thinner and thinner

until we're less than a mist,
lighter than gravity,

floating,
almost zero on the number line,

adrift but still something,
still stuck here.

Brandon Young

Held Me Green and Dying

Title a line from Dylan Thomas

I admit I'm blamable, running past the middle,
running from the story of me, starting with two boys
supine on the jewel-rich lawn,

I'll be the boy and you'll be the girl, he said,
and seemed to absorb me—cracked me open
with his hands, the way hands do,

that spanned the shape of us and the backyard.
Every now and then I'd tell it this way:
the day of the bright-blond boy and me,

shamed suddenly that there was something
I hungered after, something more. More than
green grass. It had to do with our bodies.

This story I liked least, so for years
I refused it and eventually forgot what happened.
I'd skip the part when we kiss. We kissed

near the trees, the flowers, then afterward imagined
our other story, and played house, the green
from time or rot or Eden seeping into us.

A Victorian woman's story ended this way:
everything I see is green. I believe her.
She was poisoned by wearing dresses

dyed with arsenic because it made them insatiably
emerald. She was beautiful, sheathed verdant, afraid
of what she had let it do to her.

Our other story was learning how to tell it, hand
in hand with each other—went unsaid. We were unfaceable,
sprawled, gripped together, even when the logic

alludes me. We weren't in love—we pretended to be,
pursued by all that green, pursued by all my stories
because I never ran from the end:

I put on my grandmother's dress, another hidden
green and spun, watched it all flare around me.
He watched too, then brought me flowers.

It didn't kill me—I didn't die, from green, or anything
budding, despite what I expected. I think now
of things that were once green and aren't,

those that could be and can't,
things that are green and shouldn't:
the whites of the Victorian woman's eyes,

her body tender, brokendown from arsenic,
flowing into a desire I can hardly blame, the desire
felt for all her gowns, hues—she is held

emerald, olive, moss, jaded, unfaded within me
and the bright-blond boy. We played house.
We dressed. We touched. Became insatiable.

Emily Zogbi

I Help Lara Croft With Her First Kill

in high definition / I can watch her / get mauled by
a bear / a mountain lion / a man / impaled on
a loose piece of metal / a tree branch / a spike
protruding from the ground / drowned in
a river / the ocean / a shallow puddle
of mud / it doesn't matter how
\/
it happens / every time / she
screams / moans / grunts / gasps / she
makes it fun / makes me want
to hear the squelch / as she's sliced apart by
an airplane propeller / a boat propeller
a chopper's static wing
\/
I've spent a lot of time / with her / Me + Lara
build a fire / Me + Lara
learn to / see in the dark / be invisible / weep
in private / light a funeral pyre / Me + Lara
learn to / be an animal / go into caves
full of / wolves / come back
\/
changed / ravenous / when he / grabs us / his hand
slithers up our / arm / engulfs our / chin / we know
to / reel back / go for the eyes and / dig / gnash and
grab / anything solid / smash / smash / smash / not stop
till his skull is / a shattered teapot / Lara
retches / turns to the sky / cries
\/
oh god as in / there is no turning back
oh god as in / I had no choice
oh god as in / this was going to happen anyway

\/
in the beginning / Lara is / trapped / crawling
towards / daylight / she's dirty
and broken / and bursts
through the earth / I think
she's not gonna make it / then
she does

CONTRIBUTORS' NOTES

ENDRE ADY (1877-1919, Hungary) was a breakthrough artist in Hungarian poetry who filled formal verse with contemporary language and contents, fighting the vestiges of feudalism at the turn of the century. He simply called his first book *New Poems* (1906); his last book, *Leading the Dead* (1918), contains anti-war poems.

KELLI RUSSELL AGODON's fourth collection of poems is *Dialogues with Rising Tides* (Copper Canyon Press, 2021). She is the cofounder of Two Sylvias Press and the co-director of Poets on the Coast: A Weekend Retreat for Women. You can write to her directly at kelli@agodon.com or visit her website: agodon.com.

ANTHONY AGUERO is a queer writer in Los Angeles, CA. His work has appeared in the *Bangalore Review*, *2River View*, *The Acentos Review*, and *The Temz Review*.

RENNIE AMENT's poetry has appeared in *West Branch*, *Minnesota Review*, *Bat City Review*, *Sixth Finch*, and *Colorado Review*, among others. She is the runner-up for the Erskine J. Poetry Prize from Smartish Pace (2019), winner of the Yellowwood Prize in Poetry from *Yalobusha Review* (2018), a finalist for the Anzaldúa Poetry Prize (2018), and a nominee for both the Pushcart Prize and *Best New Poets*. She lives in New York City and online at rennieament.com.

YVONNE AMEY is a poet living in the Southeast. Her work has appeared in *Tin House*, *Pleiades*, *Hobart*, and elsewhere. Her microchapbook, *Little Debbies*, is published by The Origami Poetry Project.

BECK ANSON (he/they) is a queer and trans emerging writer whose work weaves together gender, sexuality, and mental health. His work can be found in *Humana Obscura* and *Rattle*. He holds two degrees in botany and lives in Burlington, VT.

ROSE AUSLANDER lives on Cape Cod and is addicted to water and poetry (not necessarily in that order). Look for her book, *Wild Water Child*; her chapbooks *Folding Water*, *Hints*, and *The Dolphin in the Gowanus*; and her poems in the *Berkeley Poetry Review*, *Tupelo Quarterly*, *Tinderbox*, and *Rumble Fish*.

WALE AYINLA is a Nigerian writer. His works recently appeared or are forthcoming in *Guernica* and *South Dakota Review*. He is a staff reader for *Adroit Journal*. His full-length manuscript, *Sea Blues on Water Meridian*, was a finalist for the inaugural CAAPP Book Prize.

JAMAICA BALDWIN hails from Santa Cruz, CA, by way of Seattle. Her poetry has appeared, or is forthcoming, in *Prairie Schooner*, *Guernica*, *The Missouri Review*, *Adroit*, and *TriQuarterly*, among others. She is a 2021 National Endowment for the Arts Fellow and the 2019 winner of the San Miguel de Allende Writers Conference Contest in Poetry. Her work has been supported by Hedgebrook, Furious Flower, and the Jack Straw Writers Program. She lives in Nebraska where she is pursuing her PhD in English at University of Nebraska-Lincoln. jamaicabaldwin.com.

ABBIGAIL BALDYS is an interdisciplinary artist. Her poetry has appeared in *Collision*, *Three Rivers Review*, *491 Magazine*, *Reality Beach*, *Anomaly*, and elsewhere. She earned her MFA from Saint Mary's College of California and was recently a resident at Vermont Studio Center.

MARIE-CLAIRE BANCQUART (1932–2019) was a French poet, novelist, and literary critic. A resident of Paris, Bancquart was a professor of contemporary French literature at the Sorbonne. She authored over 30 collections of poetry and several novels. These poems come from her 1988 collection *Opéra des limites* (José Corti).

CAROLINE BARNES has published poetry in *Rattle*, *Unbroken Journal*, and *American Journal of Poetry*. She lives in the Washington, DC area and is the managing editor of a science journal for middle school teachers.

GABRIELLA BEDETTI studied translation at the University of Iowa and the Sewanee Writers' Conference. Her translations of Meschonnic's essays and other writings have appeared in *New Literary History*, *Critical Inquiry*, and *Diacritics*. Meschonnic was a guest of the MLA at her roundtable with Ralph Cohen and Susan Stewart.

FRANCESCA BELL is the author of *Bright Stain* (Red Hen Press, 2019) and a finalist for the Julie Suk Award and the Washington State Book Award. Her poems and translations appear in journals such as *B O D Y*, *New Ohio Review*, *Mid-American Review*, *Prairie Schooner*, and *Rattle*.

MONICA BERLIN is the author of *Elsewhere, That Small*, *Nostalgia for a World Where We Can Live*, and with Beth Marzoni, co-author of *No Shape Bends the River So Long*. A professor at Knox College in Galesburg, Illinois, she currently serves as associate director of the Program in Creative Writing.

SHEILA BLACK is the author of four poetry collections, most recently *Iron, Ardent* (Educe Press, 2017). A fifth collection, *Vivisection*, is forthcoming from Salmon Poetry. She is a co-editor of *Beauty is a Verb: The New Poetry of Disability* (Cinco Puntos Press, 2011). Her poems have appeared in *Poetry*, *Sugar House Review*, *The Spectacle*, *The New York Times*, and other places. She lives in San Antonio, TX, and works at AWP.

ADRIAN BLEVINS is the author of *Appalachians Run Amok; Live from the Homesick Jamboree; The Brass Girl Brouhaha;* two chapbooks; and the co-edited *Walk Till the Dogs Get Mean: Meditations on the Forbidden from Contemporary Appalachia.* She is the recipient of awards including a Wilder Prize from Two Sylvias Press, a Kate Tufts Discovery Award, and a Rona Jaffe Writer's Foundation Award. She is a professor of English at Colby College in Waterville, Maine.

DON BOES is the author of *Good Luck With That, Railroad Crossing,* and *The Eighth Continent,* selected by A. R. Ammons for the Samuel French Morse Poetry Prize. His poems have appeared in *The Louisville Review, Painted Bride Quarterly, Prairie Schooner, CutBank, Zone 3,* and *The Cincinnati Review.*

SARAH BROWNING is the author of *Killing Summer* and *Whiskey in the Garden of Eden.* She is co-founder and for 10 years was executive director of Split This Rock: Poems of Provocation & Witness. She's pursuing an MFA in poetry and creative non-fiction at Rutgers-Camden. For more info: sarahbrowning.net.

CHRIS CAMPANIONI is the author of six books, including *A and B and Also Nothing* (Otis Books | Seismicity Editions, 2020), a re-writing of Henry James's *The American* and Gertrude Stein's "Americans" which merges theory, fiction, and autobiography. Recent work appears in *Ambit, Nat. Brut,* and *American Poetry Review,* and has been translated into Spanish and Portuguese.

BERNARD CAPINPIN is a poet and translator. He is currently working on a translation of Ramon Guillermo's *Ang Makina ni Mang Turing.* He resides in Quezon City, Philippines.

SARAH CARSON's poetry and other writing have appeared in *Diagram, Guernica, The Minnesota Review, New Ohio Review,* and others. She lives in Michigan with her daughter and two dogs.

ANNE CHAMPION is the author of *She Saints & Holy Profanities* (Quarterly West, 2019), *The Good Girl is Always a Ghost* (Black Lawrence Press, 2018), *Book of Levitations* (Trembling Pillow Press, 2019), *Reluctant Mistress* (Gold Wake Press, 2013), and *The Dark Length Home* (Noctuary Press, 2017). Her work appears in *Verse Daily, Tupelo Quarterly, Prairie Schooner, Crab Orchard Review, Salamander, Redivider, PANK,* and elsewhere. anne-champion.com

SEAN CHO A. is an MFA candidate at the University of California Irvine. His work can be ignored or future-found in *Salt Hill, The Portland Review, Hobart,* and elsewhere. He is a staff reader for *Ploughshares.* In the summer of 2019 he was a Mary K. Davis scholarship recipient for the Bear River Writing Conference. Sean's manuscript *Not Bilingual* was a finalist for the Write Bloody Publishing Poetry Prize. He can be found @phlat_soda.

LISA COMPO has a BA in Creative Writing from Salisbury University and is a poetry reader for *Quarterly West*. She has work forthcoming or recently published in journals such as: *Puerto del Sol*, *Crab Orchard Review*, *Poet Lore*, and elsewhere. She was a semi-finalist for the 2019 Pablo Neruda Prize for Poetry.

BRITNY CORDERA is a Black writer and Creole poet, descending from African, Indigenous, and French/Spanish ancestors. She was a finalist for the 2020 *Narrative* 30 Below contest. Cordera's poetry can be found or is forthcoming in *RHINO*, *Narrative*, *Xavier Review*, and *Auburn Avenue*. She is an MFA candidate at Southern Illinois University in Carbondale, a teaching artist through St. Louis Poetry Center, and poetry editor at *The New Southern Fugitives*.

PHILLIP J. COZZI is a pulmonary physician living in Chicago with his wife and four children. He has had over 40 poems published in medical journals and recently was featured in *The Eloquent Poem* (Persea Press). He is working on his MFA at the School of the Art Institute of Chicago.

CURTIS L. CRISLER was born and raised in Gary, Indiana. Crisler has five full-length poetry books, two YA books, and five poetry chapbooks. He's been published in a variety of magazines, journals, and anthologies. Crisler is a Professor of English at Purdue University Fort Wayne (PFW) in Fort Wayne, Indiana.

JESSICA CUELLO is the author of *Liar*, selected by Dorianne Laux for the 2020 Barrow Street Book Prize and forthcoming in 2021. She is also the author of *Hunt* (The Word Works, 2017) and *Pricking* (Tiger Bark Press, 2016). She has been awarded the 2017 CNY Book Award, The 2016 Washington Prize, *New Letters* Poetry Prize, a Saltonstall Fellowship, and *New Ohio Review* Poetry Prize.

LEIA DARWISH is a poet, editor, copywriter, and writing instructor based in Richmond, Virginia. She studied creative writing at University of Colorado Denver and Virginia Commonwealth University. Past editorial positions include *Copper Nickel* and *Blackbird*. Her poetry and nonfiction can be found in *diode*, *The Journal*, *PANK*, *The Paris-American*, and elsewhere.

MARISSA DAVIS is a poet and translator from Paducah, Kentucky, residing in Brooklyn, New York. Her poems have appeared in *The Carolina Quarterly*, *Rattle*, *The Iowa Review*, *Sundog Lit*, and *Peach Mag*, among others. Her translations have been published in *Ezra* and are forthcoming in *Mid-American Review*. Davis's first chapbook, *My Name & Other Languages I Am Learning How to Speak* (2020) won Cave Canem's 2019 Toi Derricotte and Cornelius Eady Chapbook Prize.

MAYA TEVET DAYAN is the author of a novel and two books of poetry: *Let There Be Evening. Let There Be Chaos* (2015) and *Wherever We Float, That's Home* (2018). She is the recipient of the Israeli Prime Minister award for literature for 2018. English translations of her poems have appeared in *Rattle*, *Copper Nickel*, *Hayden's Ferry Review*, *Modern Poetry in Translation*, *Asymptote*, and *The New Quarterly*.

ELISABETH REIDY DENISON is a writer and editor from Massachusetts. Her work has appeared in *Aesthetica, Bodega, Goldfish, The Tangerine, THRUSH,* and elsewhere. She lives in London.

BRANDON THOMAS DISABATINO is the author of the poetry collection *6 Weeks of White Castle /n Rust.* His work for the theater has been performed in NYC and Cincinnati. Other writing has appeared in *Painted Bride Quarterly, Columbia Journal, Juke Joint, New Limestone Review,* and other publications.

ALINE DOLINH is an MFA student in poetry at Boston University. In the past, Dolinh has served as a poetry reader and summer mentor for *The Adroit Journal.* Dolinh's work has previously been nominated for Best of the Net and appeared in publications including *Frontier Poetry, TRACK// FOUR,* and *Alien Mouth.*

CLAIRE EDER's poems and translations have appeared in *Gulf Coast, The Cincinnati Review, PANK, Midwestern Gothic,* and *Guernica,* among other publications. She holds an MFA from the University of Florida and a PhD from Ohio University. She lives in Madison, Wisconsin. Find her online at claireeder.com.

LARA EGGER is the author of *How to Love Everyone and Almost Get Away with It* (University of Massachusetts Press, 2021), which won the Juniper Prize for Poetry. Her poems have appeared in *Verse Daily, West Branch, Ninth Letter, New Ohio Review,* and elsewhere. Originally from Australia, Egger lives in Boston where she co-owns a Spanish tapas bar.

MICHAEL FRAZIER is a poet and educator. His poems appear or are forthcoming in *Cream City Review, Tokyo Poetry Journal, COUNTERCLOCK, Construction, Visible Poetry Project, Day One,* and elsewhere. He is a staff reader for *The Adroit Journal* and *Button Poetry* and a 2020 Seventh Wave editorial resident. He lives in central Japan where he's working on a poetry collection about his mother. He can talk for days about anime, poetry, and how Christ has changed his life. Follow on Twita @fraziermichael.

ELIZABETH GALOOZIS's poems have appeared in *Sundog Lit, Faultline, Mantis, Not Very Quiet, Sinister Wisdom,* and *in parentheses,* among others. Her poem "The Grove" was a finalist for the Inverted Syntax Sublingua Prize for Poetry. She works as a librarian and lives in southern California.

ADAM GIANFORCARO is the author of the poetry collection *Morning Time in the Household, Looking Out,* and the children's picture book *Uma the Umbrella.* His poems and stories can be found in *The Cincinnati Review* (miCRo series), *the minnesota review, Poet Lore, Entropy, Maudlin House,* and elsewhere.

JESSICA GOODFELLOW's books are *Whiteout* (University of Alaska Press, 2017), *Mendeleev's Mandala* (2015) and *The Insomniac's Weather Report* (2014). Her work has appeared in *Best American Poetry 2018, Scientific American, The Southern Review,* and *Verse Daily.* A former writer-in-residence at Denali National Park and Preserve, Jessica lives in Japan.

HAYLEY GRAFFUNDER is the managing editor of *Blackbird* and an MFA candidate in poetry at Virginia Commonwealth University. She is the recipient of the 2020 Catherine and Joan Byrne Poetry Prize and the 2018 Lon Otto Prize for Poetry. Her work has appeared in *Occulum*.

BENJAMIN S. GROSSBERG is the author of *My Husband Would* (University of Tampa Press, 2020) and *Sweet Core Orchard* (University of Tampa Press, 2009), and winner of the Tampa Review Prize for Poetry and a Lambda Literary Award. He directs the creative writing program at the University of Hartford.

KATHLEEN HELLEN's collection *Umberto's Night* won the Washington Writers' Publishing House prize for poetry in 2012. Her honors include the Thomas Merton Prize in Poetry and prizes from the *H.O.W. Journal* and *Washington Square Review*. Hellen's latest poetry collection is *The Only Country Was the Color of My Skin*.

AMBALILA HEMSELL is the author of *Queen in Blue*. She is an inaugural recipient of the Kundiman Sewanee Fellowship, a former writer-in-residence at InsideOut Literary Arts in Detroit, and a Pushcart nominee. Her poetry can be found in *Fairytale Review, Columbia Journal, The American Literary Review*, and elsewhere. She lives in Tacoma, Washington, with her family.

MAURA HIGH's poetry has appeared in a number of print and online journals and in a chapbook, *The Garden of Persuasions*. Maura is Welsh by birth, an editor by trade, and immigrated to America as an adult. Her other occupations? Language, nature conservation, civic activism, family, and Zen practice.

EXCELL N. HUNTER is a native of New Orleans. He had an exhibition of his visual art in Karmiel, Israel, and poetry accepted to *Every Day Poetry, Ocean Diamond, The Cherry Blossom,* and *The Pomona Valley Review;* 3rd place prize, Intl Black Writers & Artists L.A.; two Honorable Mentions at New Millenium Writings; and a 1st place prize, *Ibwala*. He is a former public elementary school teacher and owns/operates a tutoring business in Los Angeles.

KOREY HURNI was born and raised in Lansing, Michigan, and earned his MFA at Western Michigan University where he served as poetry editor for *Third Coast*. He is currently pursuing his PhD at the University of Wisconsin - Milwaukee.

ADEEKO IBUKUN is an award-winning Nigerian poet. He won the 2015 Babishai Niwe African Poetry Prize. His works are widely published or forthcoming in journals, including *Sentinel UK, Open: Journal of Arts & Letters, Salamander Magazine, 20.35 Africa, Expound,* and *Fortunate Traveler*.

REBECCA IRENE's poems are published in *Pidgeonholes, Carve Magazine, Juked, Atlanta Review*, and elsewhere. She received residencies from Monson Arts, Norton Island, and Hewnoaks. Poetry editor for *The Maine Review*, she holds an MFA in Writing from VCFA and lives in Portland, Maine, where she supports her word-addiction by waitressing.

NAZIFA ISLAM grew up in Novi, Michigan. Her poems have appeared in *Boston Review*, *Gulf Coast*, *The Believer*, and *Beloit Poetry Journal*, among other publications, and her poetry collection *Searching for a Pulse* (2013) was released by Whitepoint Press. She earned her MFA at Oregon State University. Find her @nafoopal.

KENNETH JAKUBAS holds an MFA from Western Michigan University, where he continues to serve as the assistant poetry editor for *Third Coast Magazine*. His work has appeared or is forthcoming in *The Atlanta Review*, *Birdcoat Quarterly*, *The Los Angeles Review*, *Zone 3*, *Sundog Lit*, and *Midwest Review*, among others. He lives and teaches in Battle Creek, Michigan, with his wife and son.

SUSAN JOHNSON received her MFA and PhD from the University of Massachusetts Amherst, where she teaches writing. Poems of hers have recently appeared in *North American Review*, *Comstock*, *Off the Coast*, and *SLAB*. She lives in South Hadley, Massachusetts, and her commentaries can be heard on NEPM.

MICHAL "MJ" JONES is a poet, parent, and MFA graduate fellow at Mills College in Oakland, California. Their work is featured or forthcoming at *Anomaly*, *Kissing Dynamite*, and *Borderlands Texas Poetry Review*. They are an assistant poetry editor at *Foglifter Press*, and have fellowships from the Hurston/Wright Foundation, VONA/Voices, & Kearny Street Workshop.

ASEEM KAUL lives in Minneapolis and is an associate professor at the University of Minnesota. His poems have appeared in *DMQ Review*, *Eclectica*, *Blood Orange Review*, and *The Cortland Review*, among others, and he is the author of a collection of short fiction titled *études*.

ROGAN KELLY is the author of *Demolition in the Tropics* (Seven Kitchens Press, 2019) and the editor of *The Night Heron Barks*.

DAVID KEPLINGER's latest books include *Another City* (Milkweed Editions, 2018), which was awarded the 2019 Rilke Prize, and *The Long Answer* (Texas A&M, 2020), a selection of his poems over the last twenty years. In 2020 he received the Emily Dickinson Award from the Poetry Society of America. He lives in Washington D.C. and teaches at American University.

CHRIS KETCHUM is a poet from northern Idaho. He is the Curb Creative Writing Fellow at Vanderbilt University, where he has served as a poetry editor for *Nashville Review*. His poems have appeared or are forthcoming in *Beloit Poetry Journal*, *Five Points*, *New Ohio Review*, *Tar River Poetry*, and elsewhere.

ASHLEY SOJIN KIM is an MFA candidate in poetry at the University of Florida. She received her BA in Writing Seminars from The Johns Hopkins University and is originally from Los Angeles. Her work has appeared in *Faultline Journal of Arts and Letters*.

KATHLEEN KIRK is the author of eight poetry chapbooks, the poetry editor for *Escape Into Life*, an online magazine, and a former editor of *RHINO*. Her poem "Death of a Sasquatch" quotes Linda Loman from *Death of a Salesman* by Arthur Miller and owes a debt to cryptozoology as well.

EMILIE KNEIFEL is a poet/critic, editor at *The Puritan/Theta Wave*, creator of *CATCH/PLAYD8s*, and also a list (dovedovedove). find 'em at emiliekneifel.com, @emiliekneifel, and in Tiohtiá:ke, hopping and hoping.

SUSANNA LANG's third collection of poems, *Travel Notes from the River Styx*, was published by Terrapin Books in 2017, and her chapbook, *Self-Portraits*, was released by Blue Lyra Press in August, 2020. Her poems and translations have appeared in *The Literary Review* and *The Slowdown*, among other publications.

SCOT LANGLAND is a queer poet who grew up in Alabama. He now happily resides in Fayetteville as an MFA candidate in poetry at the University of Arkansas. His poetry has appeared, or is forthcoming, in *Best New Poets 2018*, *Bayou Magazine*, *Poetry South*, and *Waccamaw*, among others.

MARIANA LIN has an MFA in poetry from Pacific University and was nominated by Marvin Bell for Best New Poets 2019. Her poems have been finalists for awads like *The Mississippi Review* Prize and *Arts & Letters* Rumi Poetry Prize. Her other writing has appeared in *The Paris Review*, *New York Magazine*, *Huffington Post*, and others.

CHRISTOPHER LOCKE's poems have appeared in *The North American Review*, *Poetry East*, *Verse Daily*, *Southwest Review*, *32 Poems*, *The Sun*, *Rattle*, *West Branch*, *The Night Heron Barks*, and many others. *25 Trumbulls Road* won the Black River Chapbook Competition (Black Lawrence Press) and was released in early 2020.

ANTHONY THOMAS LOMBARDI is a poet and former music journalist. His work has appeared or is forthcoming in *Wildness*, *Third Coast*, *Gigantic Sequins*, *American Poetry Journal*, *Dialogist*, *Tahoma Literary Review*, *Salamander*, *Permafrost*, and elsewhere. A recipient of a scholarship from the Shipman Agency, he serves as a poetry reader and contributor for *The Adroit Journal* and lives in Brooklyn, New York, with his cat, Dilla.

TARA MESALIK MACMAHON's first collection, *Barefoot Up the Mountain*, won the 2020 Open Country Press chapbook contest and is due out in late 2021. Her poems appear or are forthcoming in *Nimrod International Journal*, Red Hen Press's *New Moons*, *Cold Mountain Review*, *Dogwood: A Journal of Poetry and Prose*, *Duende*, and others. She was a finalist for the Dogwood Poetry Prize and *Nimrod*'s Francine Ringold Award for New Writers.

ANGIE MACRI is the author of *Underwater Panther* (Southeast Missouri State University) and winner of the Cowles Poetry Book Prize. Her recent work appears in *Inkwell*, *Quarterly West*, and *Sou'Wester*. An Arkansas Arts Council fellow, she lives in Hot Springs and teaches at Hendrix College.

ELIZABETH MAJERUS is a poet, musician, and English teacher, and she lives in Urbana, Illinois, with her family. Her poems have been published most recently in *Arsenic Lobster, Another Chicago Magazine*, and *The Madison Review*. She is one-third of the band Motes.

ROBERT MCDONALD's work has appeared previously in *Columbia Poetry Review, Sentence, Court Green, PANK*, and *Escape Into Life*, among many other journals and zines. McDonald lives in Chicago and works at an independent bookstore. "Irruption" is from a manuscript in progress.

STEVE MCDONALD's poetry has appeared in numerous journals. His second book, *Credo*, was a finalist in the Brick Road Poetry competition, and his chapbook *Golden Fish / Dark Pond* won the *Comstock Review* Chapbook Contest. A two-time Pushcart Prize nominee, he has received awards from *Tupelo Press, Tiferet, Nimrod*, and others.

T. J. MCLEMORE is the author of the chapbook *circle/square* (Autumn House, 2020). His poems appear in *New England Review, Crazyhorse, 32 Poems, The Adroit Journal, SLICE, Poetry Daily, Best New Poets*, and other publications. McLemore is currently a doctoral student in environmental humanities at the University of Colorado Boulder.

CLAIRE MCQUERRY's poems have appeared in *Tin House, Poetry Northwest, Waxwing Literary Journal, Birmingham Poetry Review*, and other journals. Her poetry collection *Lacemakers* won the Crab Orchard First Book Prize. She is an assistant professor at Bradley University.

JANE MEDVED is the author of *Deep Calls To Deep* (winner of the Many Voices Project, New Rivers Press, 2017) and the chapbook *Olam, Shana, Nefesh*. Recent essays and poems have appeared in *The Seneca Review, Guesthouse, Juked, Gulf Coast On-Line*, and *The Tampa Review*. Her translations of Hebrew poetry can be seen in *Hayden's Ferry, Copper Nickel*, and *Cagibi*. She is poetry editor of the *Ilanot Review* and a visiting lecturer at Bar Ilan University.

DAVID MELVILLE's poems have appeared in journals such as *Water~Stone Review, The Timberline Review, Pilgrimage*, and *Buddhist Poetry Review*. His poetry has also been anthologized in the college textbook *Listening to Poetry: An Introduction for Readers and Writers*. For many years he earned his living as a lawyer.

HENRI MESCHONNIC (1932–2009) is a key figure of French "new poetics." He is known worldwide as a poet, essayist, and translator of the Hebrew verse of the Bible. [all of life] appears in *L'obscur travaille* (*The Dark Works*, Arfuyen, 2012), his nineteenth and final collection of poems.

ROBIN MESSING's short story "Drive-by" was a 2011 nominee for a Pushcart Prize. She is the author of a novel, *Serpent in the Garden of Dreams*, two poetry chapbooks, *From Temporary Worker* and *Holding Not Having*, and a recently-completed novel, *When They Were Fire*.

AKSINIA MIHAYLOVA is a poet, educator, and translator of over 35 books of poetry and prose. Her six poetry books in Bulgarian have been translated into many languages. *Ciel à Perdre*, her first poetry collection written in French, received France's Prix Apollinaire in 2014. She released her second French-language collection, *Le Baiser du Temps*, in June 2019; it received the 2020 Prix Max-Jacob. Mihaylova is the founder of the literary journal *Ah, Maria* and resides in Sofia, Bulgaria.

AMY MILLER's writing has appeared in *Barrow Street, Gulf Coast, Tupelo Quarterly, Willow Springs*, and *ZYZZYVA*. Her full-length poetry collection *The Trouble with New England Girls* won the Louis Award from Concrete Wolf Press. Raised in California and Massachusetts, she now lives in Oregon.

REBECCA MORTON received an MFA in poetry from Eastern Washington University. Her work appears in *Atlanta Review, Hummingbird: Magazine of the Short Poem, Storm Cellar, The Cincinnati Review, Pacifica Literary Review, Crab Creek Review, Tupelo Quarterly, DMQ Review*, and elsewhere. She lives in Seattle with her wife and children.

MARIE MOULIN-SALLES's credentials include a Masters from Caen University, France, and an Advanced Spanish degree, Salamanca, Spain. She has been a French teacher and translator for 30 years and a translator of business documents, literary texts, simultaneous interpretation in the courtroom, voiceover projects, and live French narration with musical performance.

SIMONE MUENCH's books include *Wolf Centos* (Sarabande), *Suture* (BLP; sonnets written with Dean Rader), and others. She co-edited *They Said: A Multi-Genre Anthology of Contemporary Collaborative Writing* (BLP). A recipient of an NEA fellowship and the Kathryn A. Morton Prize, she is advisor for *Jet Fuel Review* and a poetry editor for *Tupelo Quarterly*.

JASON MYERS is editor-in-chief of *EcoTheo Review*. A candidate for holy orders in the Episcopal Diocese of Texas, his work has been a finalist in the National Poetry Series and the A. Poulin, Jr. Prize. He lives outside Austin with his wife, Allison Grace, and their son, Robinson.

KELL NELSON is a writer and artist in Phoenix. Her experimental translations have appeared in *Florida Review, Seattle Review, Anmly, Best American Experimental Writing*, and elsewhere. She's the author of two chapbooks and the recipient of a 2021 Fulbright to Japan. She teaches Interdisciplinary Studies at Arizona State University. kellnelson.com

SARAH NICHOLS lives and writes in Connecticut. She is the author of eight chapbooks, including *She May Be a Saint* (Porkbelly Press, 2019) and *Dreamland for Keeps* (Porkbelly, 2018.) Her work has appeared in *Drunk Monkeys, Kanstellation, Rogue Agent*, and many other journals.

BRIANNA NOLL is the author of *The Era of Discontent*, forthcoming from Elixir Press, and *The Price of Scarlet*, named one of the top poetry books of 2017 by the *Chicago Review of Books*. Poetry editor of *The Account*, which she helped found, she lives in Los Angeles.

COLLEEN O'BRIEN's poetry and fiction have appeared in *Fence*, *Kenyon Review Online*, *The Gettysburg Review*, *The Antioch Review*, and other journals. Her story "Charlie" won a Pushcart Prize and will appear in *Pushcart Prize XLV* in 2021. Her chapbook, *Spool in the Maze*, won the DIAGRAM/New Michigan Press Prize.

CINDY JUYOUNG OK's recent poems can be found in *Conjunctions*, *jubilat*, and *The Bennington Review*. She teaches creative writing and is assistant poetry editor at *Guernica Magazine*.

SARA LUPITA OLIVARES is the author of *Migratory Sound*, winner of the 2020 CantoMundo Poetry Prize, and *Field Things* (dancing girl press). She earned her PhD at Western Michigan University and works as an assistant professor of English at New Mexico Highlands University.

CHRISTINA OLSON's most recent chapbook, *The Last Mastodon*, won the Rattle 2019 Chapbook Contest. She is an associate professor of creative writing at Georgia Southern University and tweets about coneys and mastodons as @olsonquest. Her website is thedrevlow-olsonshow.com.

PABLO OTAVALO is from Cuenca, Ecuador and now lives and writes in Illinois. A recipient of the 2013 & 2014 Illinois Emerging Poet prize, his work has appeared in *RHINO*, *Jet Fuel Review*, *Structo Magazine*, *Ninth Letter*, *Glass Poetry Journal*, *Tupelo Press*, *Levitate*, and *No Tender Fences: Anthology of Immigrant & First-Generation American Poetry*. We must find what we revere in each other.

RACHELLE PARKER is a writer. She was selected winner of the Furious Flower Poetry Prize and 3rd in the Allen Ginsberg Poetry Award. Her work appears in *About Place Journal*, *The Adirondack Review*, *Paterson Literary Review*, and the anthology *The BreakBeat Poets Volume 2: Black Girl Magic*.

GENEVIEVE PAYNE received her MFA in poetry from Syracuse University where she was the 2019 recipient of the Leonard Brown Prize in poetry. Her work is forthcoming in *Colorado Review* and *Up the Staircase Quarterly*.

CECILIA PINTO's work has appeared in a variety of journals, most recently *Change Seven*, *Orca*, and *Coffin Bell*. Cecilia would like to acknowledge her debt to Susan Moran for generously giving her the first line of the poem, 'Nurse.'

MEGAN PINTO has received scholarships from Bread Loaf and the Port Townsend Writers' Conference, and an Amy Award from Poets & Writers. Her poems have been published in *Ploughshares*, *Lit Hub*, *AAWW's The Margins*, and elsewhere. She holds an MFA in Poetry from Warren Wilson.

SUSAN AZAR PORTERFIELD has three books of poetry: *In the Garden of Our Spines*, *Kibbe*, and *Dirt, Root, Silk* (Cider Press Review Editor's Prize). Poems have appeared in *The Georgia Review*, *Barrow Street*, *Mid-American Review*, *Crab Orchard Review*, *RHINO*, *Puerto del Sol*, *Poetry Ireland Review*, and *Ambit*.

MEG REYNOLDS is a poet, artist, and teacher living in Burlington, Vermont. Her work has appeared in *Mid-American Review*, *Sixth Finch*, *The Offing*, and the anthologies *Monster Verse: Poems Human and Inhuman*, *The Book of Donuts*, and *With You: Withdrawn Poems of the #Metoo Movement*.

RAINER MARIA RILKE was an influential German-language poet and novelist who died in 1926. His most well-known works include *Duino Elegies*, *Sonnets to Orpheus*, and the postumously-published *Letters to a Young Poet*. "Buddha" originally appeared in Rilke's collection *New Poems (Neue Gedichte)*, published in 1907.

LIANA SAKELLIOU has published 18 books of poetry, criticism, and translation in Greece, the USA, and France. She teaches American literature, specializing in contemporary poetry, and creative writing in the Department of English Language and Literature of the University of Athens. She has received grants from the Fulbright Foundation and others.

STEWART SHAW is a librarian, poet, writer, and author of the chapbook *The House of Men*. His poems have been published in *African American Review*, *Imagoes: A Queer Anthology*; *Split this Rock: Poems of Resistance, Power & Resilience*; *Serendipity*; and others, as well as short stories in *Mighty Real: An Anthology of African American Same Gender Loving Writing* and *African Voices*. He is a Pushcart nominated poet and a Cave Canem Poetry Fellow.

DON SCHOFIELD has been living and writing in Greece since 1980. A citizen of both his homeland and his adopted country, he has published several poetry collections, the most recent of which are *The Flow of Wonder* (2018) and *In Lands Imagination Favors* (2014). His first book, *Approximately Paradise*, was a finalist for the Walt Whitman Award, and his translations have been nominated for a Pushcart Prize and the Greek National Translation Award.

CARRIE SHIPERS's poems have appeared in *Crab Orchard Review*, *Hayden's Ferry Review*, *New England Review*, *North American Review*, *Prairie Schooner*, *The Southern Review*, and other journals. She is the author of *Ordinary Mourning* (ABZ, 2010), *Cause for Concern* (Able Muse, 2015), *Family Resemblances* (University of New Mexico, 2016), and *Grief Land* (University of New Mexico, 2020).

SARAH DICKENSON SNYDER has three poetry collections, *The Human Contract*, *Notes from a Nomad* (nominated for the Massachusetts Book Awards 2018), and *With a Polaroid Camera* (2019). She has been a 30/30 poet for Tupelo Press and nominated for Best of the Net in 2017. Recent work has appeared in *Rattle*, *Artemis*, *The Sewanee Review*, and *RHINO*. sarahdickensonsnyder.com

PAUL SOHAR came to the US as a Hungarian student refugee. Since then he has published seventeen books of translations and three of his own poetry, the last one being *In Sun's Shadow* (Ragged Sky Press, Princeton, 2020). Magazine publications: *Agni*, *Rattle*, *RHINO*, *Seneca Review*, and numerous others.

JENNIFER SPERRY STEINORTH is a poet, educator, interdisciplinary artist and licensed builder. The author of *A Wake with Nine Shades* (2019) and *Her Read: A Graphic Poem* (2021), she has received grants from Vermont Studio Center, the Sewanee Writers Conference, and the MFA for Writers at Warren Wilson College.

NOAH STETZER is the author of *Because I Can See Needing a Knife* (Red Bird Chapbooks). His poems have appeared in *Sixth Finch*, *The Cortland Review*, *Hobart*, and other journals. Noah can be found online at noahstetzer.com.

KELI STEWART's work has appeared in *Quiddity*, *Meridians*, *Warpland*, *Hip Mama*, *Calyx*, and elsewhere. She received artist fellowships from Hedgebrook and the Augusta Savage Gallery Arts International Residency. Keli's work was selected for first place in the Gwendolyn Brooks Poetry Award from the Illinois Center of the Book. Her manuscript *After Birth* was recently named semi-finalist for the Claudia Emerson Chapbook Award.

STEPHANIE LANE SUTTON writes poetry, essays, and fiction. She is the author of *Shiny Insect Sex* (Bull City Press), a chapbook of flash fiction. Her writing has appeared in *The Adroit Journal*, *Black Warrior Review*, *The Offing*, and *DIALOGIST*, among others. Find her online at stephanielanesutton.com or tweeting @AthenaSleepsIn.

JASON TANDON is the author of four books of poetry including *The Actual World* (Black Lawrence Press, 2019). His poems have appeared in many journals and magazines, including *Ploughshares*, *Prairie Schooner*, *Beloit Poetry Journal*, *North American Review*, and *Esquire*. He is a senior lecturer in the Arts & Sciences Writing Program at Boston University.

LEE COLIN THOMAS lives and writes in Minneapolis, MN. His poems have appeared in *Poet Lore*, *Salamander*, *The Gay and Lesbian Review Worldwide*, *Water~Stone Review*, *Midwestern Gothic*, *Pilgrimage*, *The Nassau Review*, *Narrative Magazine*, and elsewhere. Online at leecolinthomas.net.

CEDRIC TILLMAN holds a BA in English from UNC Charlotte and graduated from American University's Creative Writing MFA program. His debut collection, *Lilies in the Valley*, was published by Willow Books in 2013. His latest offering, *In My Feelins*, was published by WordTech in 2019. He currently lives in northern Virginia.

RODRIGO TOSCANO's *The Charm and The Dread* is due in 2021 (Fence Books). He is the author of ten books of poetry, including a National Poetry Series selection. He works for the Labor Institute and NIH on research projects dealing with Covid-19. Toscano lives in New Orleans.

JESS TURNER is a poet from Pittsburgh. Currently, she is an MFA candidate at Colorado State University, where she received the 2020 Academy of American Poets Prize. She is the managing editor for *Colorado Review*. Her own poems can be found in *Pleiades*, *Salt Hill Journal*, and *New Delta Review*.

STEPHEN TUTTLE's fiction and prose poetry has appeared in *The Threepenny Review, The Southern Review, The Gettysburg Review, The Normal School, Hayden's Ferry Review,* and elsewhere. He teaches creative writing and American literature at Brigham Young University.

ENRIQUE S. VILLASIS is a poet and a scriptwriter born in Milagros, Masbate, Philippines. He has received numerous national literary awards for his poems. His first book of poems, *Agua*, was a finalist for a National Book Award. He is a member of Linangan sa Imahen, Retorika, at Anyo. He lives in Quezon City and currently writes television shows for ABS-CBN.

SARA MOORE WAGNER lives in West Chester, Ohio, and is the recipient of a 2019 Sustainable Arts Foundation award and the author of the chapbooks *Tumbling After* (Red Bird Chapbooks, 2021) and *Hooked Through* (2017). Her poetry has appeared or is forthcoming in *Cimarron, Third Coast, Poet Lore,* and *Waxwing,* among others. She has been nominated multiple times for the Pushcart Prize and Best of the Net. Find her at saramoorewagner.com.

JACKIE K. WHITE, former professor of English at Lewis University, served as an assistant editor for *They Said: A Multi-Genre Anthology of Collaborative Writing*. Other publications include three chapbooks of poetry and the collaborative chapbook, *Hex & Howl*, co-written with Simone Muench, forthcoming from Black Lawrence Press, 2021.

DONALD MACE WILLIAMS is a retired newspaper writer-editor and also a former professor. His book *Wolfe and Other Poems* was published in 2017 by Wundor Editions. His four prose books include a pastoral novel, *The Sparrow and the Hall*, set in seventh-century Northumbria. He lives in the Texas Panhandle.

JOHN SIBLEY WILLIAMS is the author of *As One Fire Consumes Another* (Orison Poetry Prize), *Skin Memory* (Backwaters Prize), and *Summon* (JuxtaProse Chapbook Prize). A twenty-six-time Pushcart nominee and winner of various awards, John serves as editor of *The Inflectionist Review*, founder of Caesura Poetry Workshop, and is a literary agent.

DANIEL WOODY was born in Los Angeles, raised in Las Vegas, educated in Chicago, and now lives in Shanghai where he teaches in the Writing Program at NYU Shanghai. His poetry can be found in *The Journal Petra, Chicago Review, The Volta,* and *BOAAT*.

WILLIAM WINFIELD WRIGHT is Fulbright Scholar and professor of English at Colorado Mesa University. He has published in *14 Hills, Beloit Poetry Journal, Field, The Ninth Letter, Permafrost, The Seattle Review, Third Coast,* and elsewhere. His work has been nominated for a Pushcart Prize and featured on Poetry Daily.

BRANDON YOUNG is a queer poet and current MFA candidate for poetry at Virginia Commonwealth University, where he is a copyeditor and reader for *Blackbird* literary journal. He has earned a BA in English and Creative Writing from Indiana University.

EMILY ZOGBI is a writer from Long Island. By 2021, she should have her MFA in poetry from The New School. Her poems have appeared in *Chronogram, Rumble Fish Quarterly, Tinderbox Poetry Journal, Apricity Press,* and *Blue Mountain Review*. She wishes she had been a dancer.

DONORS

Jane Fulton Alt
John Amen
Paul Austin
Francesca Bell
Nina Bell
Virginia Bell
Prudence Brown
Cherie Carson
Luisa & Aaron Caycedo-Kimura
Dan Cohen
Richard Scott Cohen
Michael Cole
P. Scott Cunningham
Nancy Davis
Bess de Farber
Cherie Duve
John & Carol H. Eding

David Eingorn
Timothy Ennis
Gail Goepfert
Ralph Hamilton
Ann Hudson
James R. Harris
Mary Hawley
Michael Horvich
David & Rochelle Jones
Kathleen Kirk
Darlene & Ludwig Krammer
Michael Landau
Ann Leamon
Michael Lenehan & Mary Williams
Elizabeth Levinson
Diane & David Lipkin
Ronald Litke & Judy Sickle
Tara Macmahon

John McCarthy
Beth McDermott
Pamela Miller
Faisal Mohyuddin
Lakshy Nair
Jorge Partida
Roger C. Pfingston
Marcia Pradzinski
Valerie Quinn
Scott Rabinowitz
Thomas W. Roby IV
& Jenene O. Ravesloot
Robert Rohm
Elena Ronquillo
Carol Sadtler
Joseph Schlesinger
Maureen Seaton

Sherry Smith
Donna Spruijt-Metz
Linda & George J. Stevenson
Chris Stoessel
Moira Sullivan
Pamela Taylor
May May Tchao
Angela Narciso Torres
Nick Tryling
John Van Wagner
Anastasia Vassos
Valerie Wallace
Shannon Winston
Andrea Witzke Slot
Jay Woolford
RM Xager

RHINO Reviews

an online zine of contemporary poetry book reviews

More than 300 reviews—and growing:

Aaron Caycedo-Kimura	*Ubasute*
Kimiko Hahn	*Foreign Bodies: Poems*
Major Jackson	*The Absurd Man*
Ross Gay	*Be Holding*
Rosebud Ben-Oni	*20 Atomic Sonnets*
Leila Chatti	*Deluge*
Eduardo C. Corral	*Guillotine*
Laden Osman	*Exiles of Eden*
Dean Young	*Solar Perplexus*
Dilruba Ahmed	*Bring Now the Angels*
Matthew Dickman	*Wonderland*
Carl Phillips	*Wild is the Wind*

…and so many more!

{10 to 12 fresh reviews per month}

Our reviewers are published poets, teachers, avid readers, and poetry lovers. As with our journal, we seek to create a space that is diverse, representative, inclusive, and free. Send queries to editors@rhinopoetry.org.

rhinopoetry.org/reviews